Praise for previous editions:

"*A wonderful book for those ready to move beyond the theoretical connections between psychology and sport and forward into application . . . Readers with a foundation in sport psychology will find this an excellent next stop to move beyond research and theory and into application and assessment. Summing Up: Recommended.*"

– R.E. Osborne, Texas State University-San Marcos, in *CHOICE*, January 2014

Pure Sport "*provides clear and understandable guidelines for athletes who wish to apply these techniques in their everyday routine.*"

– Andreas Stenling, Idrottsforum

"*As an introduction to basic sport psychology, this book serves as essential reading for researchers, psychologists, athletes, coaches, or just the interested reader.*"

– Andrew J. Wawrzyniak, *The Psychologist*

Pure Sport

Pure Sport is a practical guide that provides insights on asserting positive mindsets, realising potential, remaining resilient against setbacks and using these experiences to move on to greater success. The book follows the journey of the athlete through six clear steps, creating a logical framework for applied sport psychology or a path you can follow in your own practice.

This third edition is fully updated and now more accessible than ever, including new advice on maintaining a resilient attitude and taking care of athletes' mental well-being. Drawing on decades of both practical and theoretical knowledge, the authors deliver practical advice with a thorough grounding in sport psychology, supplemented by case studies, reflection questions, common problems and effective solutions, and useful summaries of key points.

Pure Sport is essential reading for all those actively involved and interested in sport, from sports psychologists and academics, to athletes and coaches.

John Kremer runs his own successful consultancy business, having been a Reader in Psychology at Queen's University Belfast for 31 years. Along with his academic interest in sport and exercise psychology he has worked directly with a wide range of national and international athletes and teams in over 50 sports.

Aidan Moran is a Professor of Cognitive Psychology at University College Dublin. A Fulbright Scholar, he has written many scientific papers on mental imagery and attention in athletes. He has advised many of Ireland's leading professional athletes and teams, including golfer Pádraig Harrington and the Irish rugby team.

Ciarán J. Kearney is an independent applied psychologist specialising in performance improvement, accountability, team culture and mental health. He has consulted widely as a performance manager in a range of sports including Gaelic games where he has worked with All-Ireland winning teams and All-Star players.

Pure Sport

Sport Psychology in Action

Third Edition

John Kremer, Aidan Moran
and Ciarán J. Kearney

Routledge
Taylor & Francis Group

LONDON AND NEW YORK

Third edition published 2019
by Routledge
2 Park Square, Milton Park, Abingdon, Oxon, OX14 4RN

and by Routledge
52 Vanderbilt Avenue, New York, NY 10017

Routledge is an imprint of the Taylor & Francis Group, an informa business

First edition published by Routledge 2008
Second edition published by Routledge 2013

British Library Cataloguing-in-Publication Data
A catalogue record for this book is available from the British Library

Library of Congress Cataloging-in-Publication Data
Names: Kremer, John, 1956– author. | Moran, Aidan P., author.
Title: Pure sport : sport psychology in action/John Kremer, Aidan Moran and
    Ciaråan Kearney.
Description: Third Edition. | New York : Routledge, 2019. | "Second edition
    published by Routledge 2013"—T.p. verso. | Includes bibliographical
    references and index.
Identifiers: LCCN 2018058887 | ISBN 9781138484009 (hardback) |
    ISBN 9781138484061 (paperback) | ISBN 9781351053181 (eBook)
Subjects: LCSH: Sports—Psychological aspects.
Classification: LCC GV706.4 .K744 2019 | DDC 796.01/9—dc23
LC record available at https://lccn.loc.gov/2018058887

ISBN: 978-1-138-48400-9 (hbk)
ISBN: 978-1-138-48406-1 (pbk)
ISBN: 978-1-351-05318-1 (ebk)

Typeset in Galliard
by Apex CoVantage, LLC

To sport.

Contents

Preface

Welcome to this, our third edition of *Pure Sport*, an edition that we have redrafted, restructured and updated significantly in order to reflect on the much changed world of sport since we last committed pen to paper in 2013. Sport has witnessed a great deal of change in the intervening years. Some of these changes (such as increased focus on mental health issues) have been for the better while others (e.g. a *win at all costs* approach) raise concerns as to where modern day professional sport may be heading – and what could be lost, damaged or hurt in the process.

Without question the resources that are now available to help sportspeople realise their potential have never been more plentiful, and the material rewards for those who succeed are extraordinary in comparison with those achieved by previous generations. Unfortunately these benefits are counterbalanced by what can attach to a philosophy where *winning at all costs* can too easily become accepted wisdom.

In this new environment, the need for measured guidance has never been greater and it was with this in mind that we chose to restructure the book around a journey, your sporting journey.

In essence *Pure Sport* is presented as your guidebook on this journey, wherever your travels may take you and whatever you may encounter along the way. Many of the themes may have made an appearance in the two earlier editions of the book but here we have tried to distil this information into more bite-size chunks and to repackage it in a digestible way that can help you to realise your sporting potential, while at the same time arming you against the pitfalls of modern sport.

In this new edition our own principles have not changed. We have tried to make sport psychology accessible and practical to those with little background in the subject. Along the way we hope to have stripped away some of the mystique that can serve to confuse the unwary. At heart, sport psychology is not hard – it is simply the way that the mind affects our physical performance. The hard part is steering a path through all the available information that is out there, and putting the useful parts together in a coherent package, with you at the helm throughout.

Pure Sport may be useful as a guide but our ultimate goal is to empower you to a point where you take charge but, this time, armed with the right knowledge, insight and skills to allow your head and body to continue to work together in complete harmony. With this in mind, your sporting journey may be eventful, at times unpredictable, but it should be embarked on with enthusiasm and optimism as you continue to explore the limits of your sporting prowess.

The response to the earlier editions of *Pure Sport* has been extremely positive but if we have learned anything from sport it is never to rest on our laurels. Instead we have endeavoured to move forward with this new edition, to see whether this reworking may help to make the material even more readable to sportspeople generally, of any age and of any level of ability. To echo our earlier attempts, we leave it up to you to decide whether or not we have succeeded – but we sincerely hope you enjoy the journey. We have.

John, Aidan and Ciarán
February 2019

Box key

	Ask yourself
	Overcoming obstacles
	Try for yourself
	Self-assessment exercise
	Case study
	Summary

1

Planning ahead

Welcome to this, your unique journey through the amazing world of sport. Make no mistake, this is likely to be a trip with many twists, turns and unexpected surprises along the way but which at heart has a very simple goal – to help you to fully explore your sporting potential.

As you start to plan this exciting journey please be aware that you will be moving through a world that is a million miles removed from that familiar to past generations. It is one where science and technology now allow sportspeople to take their bodies to the physical limits and beyond. Nowhere was this more apparent than in preparation for the 2018 FIFA World Cup where, as one example, huge efforts were spent analysing data and profiling so as to reduce the element of chance in the once dreaded penalty shootout.[1] Clearly, penalty taking is not a *lottery* but is actually a test of nerve, skill and preparation – and is one classic occasion where the mental side of sport occupies central-stage.

As athletes and coaches increasingly turn to science to find the winning edge, where does this leave sport psychology? In reality its importance has grown as the difference between winning and losing can no longer be found in a novel physical or tactical advantage. Instead, the edge can often boil down to no more than who has the mental capacity to cross the line first.

Although science has increased the predictability of sport, betting in sport has never been more popular. This is for many reasons, not least because upsets still often happen despite what the form book may say, and this is where psychology is critical. On one day you can be unbeatable, the next day your form deserts you. Your body hasn't changed dramatically in 24 hours, your fitness hasn't deserted you overnight, and all those skills that you spent hours practising haven't been for nothing – so what has changed? The answer has to be . . . your head.

Take one classic example, home advantage.[2] This is the idea that there is a performance merit attaching to playing at home. Despite the fortunes spent on preparation for professional sports, home advantage is still simply taken as a given but if you think about it for a moment, any venue effect is no more than a psychological phenomenon based on how you react to performing the same skills according to the same rules – but in different places. In other words, pure psychology at work.

Pure Sport is about going back to basics, identifying how to use psychology to your best advantage and then allowing your head to give your body the opportunity to realise its true potential. In the process we are keen to eliminate psychobabble and remove some of the mystery around the topic, thereby making sport psychology more understandable and accessible to those who really matter – people who are directly involved in sport.

By its nature sport can be fickle but there is no need to make it even more so. For example, are you only as good as your last game? Emphatically the answer is no. Simple common sense should tell you that you are actually as good as your *best* game because that was the occasion when you caught a glimpse of what you may have the potential to achieve, when the pieces of the jigsaw all came together and your true potential really shone through.

Sadly, through a conspiracy of nature and biology, the head doesn't always work to our advantage in competitive situations. In fact in some respects our heads are hard-wired to conspire *against* us, as we will explain later in the book (see *Step two*).

As one example, our natural tendency can be to label those special occasions when it did all click into place as a one-off or golden time that comes along once in a lifetime but which can't be predicted, controlled or repeated. Nothing could be further from the truth, as again we will come on to later. Indeed, unless handled with care those extraordinary occasions can sometimes become a burden we carry with us rather than a source of inspiration showing just how good we can be when, in the words of the comedian Eric Morecombe, we not only played the right notes but played them in the right order!

Using sport psychology well

On your journey, sport psychology should not be treated as a supplement but as central to your endeavour, underpinning a philosophy based on *total preparation* where absolutely nothing is left to chance or fate. Sadly in the past many people's experience of sport psychology may have been less than positive.

Once upon a time the tennis player Andy Murray was more than sceptical about the power of the mind. According to his 2006 Wimbledon blog:

> A sports psychologist handed me a book he had written. Some people think I am a bit nuts but I don't think I'm ready for a shrink just yet! I had the last laugh – I chucked the book in the bin!![3]

Many years later a significant upturn in his fortunes was accompanied by teaming up with Ivan Lendl, a coach who had come to appreciate the value of sport psychology and especially in nurturing a sense of enjoyment. So Ivan quietly set about changing Andy's mental approach, an approach that had previously emphasised sacrifice, hard work and endeavour – but sometimes at the expense of enjoyment. 'It is fun,' Lendl insisted, 'a lot of fun . . . You feel nervous, obviously. If you didn't feel nervous you'd think there was something wrong. But you have to enjoy being nervous because it's a privilege.'[4]

As another example, the five-time world champion snooker player Ronnie O'Sullivan once commented, 'I tried a sport psychologist once and I never really got anything out of it . . . if you're on, you're on; if you're off, you're off, and there's not a lot you can do about it.'[5] Sometimes referred to as *The Two Ronnies* because of his inconsistent performance profile, probably the most successful period of his career was linked to his involvement with the sport psychiatrist Professor Steve Peters, culminating in two world championship titles in 2012 and 2013.

More recently, England's success in reaching the semi-finals of the 2018 FIFA World Cup has been credited to many factors, not least the change in culture within the squad associated with the engagement of applied sport psychologist Dr Pippa Grange.

While there are numerous examples where sport psychology has been of positive value, it can also stand accused of sometimes doing more harm than good. During the 1958 football world cup finals in Sweden, the Brazilian team used the services of a sport psychologist and hypnotherapist who set about analysing pictures sketched by squad members. According to Dr Carvalhaes, one young player's efforts revealed him to be someone who was immature, lacking in fighting spirit and therefore unworthy of a starting place on the team. Fortunately Brazil's manager, Vicente Feola, chose to ignore this advice and selected the 17-year-old Pelé. The rest is history.

By this stage in our careers as sport psychologists we have been fortunate enough to work with a great many athletes across a rich variety of team and individual sports, and at every level, from grassroots to élite. Each intervention, large and small, has been invaluable in helping us to learn and accumulate a stock of knowledge that we hope can be applied across all sports and abilities.

One important lesson we have learned along the way is that there is no point in blinding people with science. Our academic credentials may be there, but they don't have to be out on public display. Instead our goal is to distil the theory of sport psychology and then transform it into manageable chunks of practical and accessible knowledge for those who are most interested in simple questions such as what to do and how to do it well.

Why *Pure Sport?*

More of the 'what and the how' later but to begin, why did we choose the title *Pure Sport?* Quite simply because that is all the book is about, purely about sport and your performance uncluttered by so much of the paraphernalia and egotistical 'stuff' (e.g. image, branding) that now surrounds sport.

Sporting times have certainly changed since the first edition of the book appeared a decade ago. In recent years we have witnessed some of the worst excesses in sport, along with casualties of an *at all costs* approach that has blighted so many sporting endeavours, and lives.

Almost daily, high profile sporting celebrities reveal the less savoury side of sport, including cheating, mental illness, depression, addiction and burnout. As the casualty list grows ever longer so perhaps there is a dawning realisation that what can become lost in the modern business of sport is the love of the game, or what we mean by 'pure sport'. With this in mind we are confident that the title is as relevant today as it ever was, if not more so.

Starting your journey

In *Pure Sport*, we argue that the most productive way for you to think about your involvement with sport is as a journey – but a journey without end, and that is why the book has been structured in the way that it has. It is noticeable how frequently the journey analogy is now used in sport. Not long after winning the BMW PGA Championship and before his remarkable victory in the 2018 Open Championship at Carnoustie in Scotland, Francesco Molinari, alongside his performance manager Dr Dave Alred, was interviewed about his approach to golf. In his own words, 'It's about always working and always improving, it's never ending. It's not just one day we'll finish because we've done it. It's never going to be done, there's always a way to get it sharper and to improve.'[6]

Before setting out on your own travels it is important to take stock, to see just where you are, what you are carrying and who you want to travel with you. As later chapters will demonstrate, *travelling light* is often the key to success, and so it's crucial to learn how and when to leave behind excess baggage that may slow you down.

At all times it is important to remember that the person who is central is the player or athlete on the journey and not those who hitch a ride or are there to offer support along the way. For example, the sport psychologist should never be more than one element of a support team that provides you with advice – but on the understanding that, over time, the role should diminish rather than grow as you gain in experience and self-reliance.

Perhaps too often in the past sport psychologists have relished the spotlight or have cast themselves as guru or 'doctor'. Such approaches are problematic, primarily because the sport psychologist works best in the background, and also because most sportspeople are not psychologically sick but are just trying to become even better at what they already do quite well. The medical model doesn't work and sets entirely the wrong tone. We feel that a more appropriate approach casts the sport psychologist as a *sport consultant* or *performance manager*, offering informed advice and support to his or her client to help realise a sporting potential.

Of course there may be occasions when problems arise that are deep-seated. At this stage it may be time to break your journey, take stock, and bring in those who are professionally competent to deal with whatever is bothering you. By way of example, excessive exercise, even addiction, can suggest a range of psychological problems linked to low self-esteem and body dissatisfaction.[7] Those psychologists with a clinical training are well qualified to identify and treat such issues, particularly when they extend to obsessive-compulsive disorders. Equally, when sport or exercise is being used inappropriately, for example to control weight or body shape, clinical psychological consequences may not be too far away.

Across the globe, it is unlikely that the demand for sport psychology has ever been higher. However, these powerful market forces can be dangerous and especially when quality control fails. In these circumstances caution must be exercised, with appropriate professional regulation required of those describing themselves as sport psychologists.

These cautions aside, without doubt sport psychology can play a part in helping you realise your physical potential – but it can never make you something that you are not. The limiting factor will always be your own physical and technical potential but fortunately the number of sportspeople who can say that they have truly explored their absolute limits remains small. As a consequence the future for sport psychology is assured. When used as part of a long-term development programme, sport psychology can help you to achieve consistent and repeatable good performances, not as a quick fix when the wheels are loose or have come off but as a measured approach to systematic performance enhancement across a sporting career or journey.

Who can benefit?

One common misconception is that sport psychology is only for the élite. Nothing could be further from the truth. Making sure that the mental and the physical work together in harmony is important for all ages and for all levels of ability with the goal of ensuring that whatever potential is there, it can be honestly explored.

There is no need to wait for experience to teach the hard lessons of sport. With careful mentoring these lessons can be imparted early in a career and a solid and enduring foundation can be built for the later years. In many respects the earlier the intervention the better because by building from the ground upwards, the person can develop both physical *and* mental skills in tandem. When these are not operating in harmony then problems can lie in store. For example, take the case where the athlete's talent starts to bring unexpected rewards. We have worked with several young athletes who find that what once came easily and lightly has now become hard work as they begin to carry the heavy burden of others' expectations on their shoulders.

To summarise, the goal of *Pure Sport* is not as obvious as you may first imagine. It is certainly not to foster dependence on a 'shrink', or to blind with science, or to build confidence to a level that is unrealistic and where disappointment is inevitable. Instead, whatever your personal ability may be, the goal of our book is to shape a sporting landscape characterised by high, broad plains of *regular and repeatable good performances.*

A word of warning here – the lofty summits of *peak performance* can be precarious. Those rare times called 'flow experiences' – when it all comes together naturally and effortlessly and without conscious thought – may occur occasionally during your journey but they can't be relied on week in, week out. Instead, a less dramatic but more realistic target to aim for is one that lies above your average performance – what is known as *repeatable good performance* (RGP). This is achievable but only as long as you remain at the head of affairs, drawing on whatever resources are necessary at whatever time and place is required, and always targeted towards the enduring goals of performance improvement and enhancement.

Lurching from event to event, and waiting for luck or fate to play its unpredictable role in affairs, is unlikely to develop *confidence*, or foster a belief in *control*, or enhance long-term *commitment*. Put simply, the healthy balancing of these three Cs best characterises a mentally strong athlete. When these three elements work together in 'harmonious interdependence' then the sport psychologist can relax and walk away with a degree of satisfaction, a job well done.

Getting your head right

It would be tempting to begin your journey by describing a magic formula for the type of head you need to succeed in sport but unfortunately life isn't that easy. For years the question of what type of personality defines a sporting champion has remained unanswered by sport psychologists. Why? The honest answer that keeps coming up is that there simply is no magic psychological formula: instead '*It depends*'.

A quick reflection on the varied characters and personalities of those who have succeeded across the wide world of sport should be enough to show you that the search for a single formula is doomed to failure. Instead, what is shaped through a combination of nature (your genes) and nurture (your experiences) is a set of characteristics and mental strategies that will help you to realise your physical potential, and to continue to *want* to realise that potential. Too many sporting careers have been blighted because someone has tried and failed to be someone who they are not. More often the answer lies closer to home – and it can be found by honestly exploring who you are, what makes you tick, and harnessing these insights to your advantage. In other words, by building *mental toughness* and *resilience*.

To some the mental strengths that are associated with sporting success can't be learnt – you either have it or you don't and it is only when the chips are really down that this reveals itself. In other words, when the going gets tough the tough get going. We fundamentally disagree with this viewpoint and firmly believe that the strength to deal with the ups and downs of a sporting career or journey can be nurtured so long as the right ingredients are brought together in the right way and at the right time, and, critically, so long as the person is willing to learn.

Sadly if we are left to our own devices then our heads don't always help. Research shows that we seem to be programmed to protect our egos at the expense of learning from our mistakes. By way of example, consider the psychology of excuses. We have a tendency to protect our egos by blaming failure on all those things that are out there and beyond our control – the pitch, the weather, our opponents, referees – while also boosting our egos by taking credit for successes, whether that is deserved or not. The good news is that if we are willing to challenge these natural inclinations (no more excuses!) then we can learn to draw on both our successes and failures in a way that strengthens character and hardens resolve for meeting future challenges.

Ultimately we believe that mental toughness should not be seen as the preserve of the fortunate few but as the right of us all. Sadly it is often true that those athletes who are most resistant to these messages are often those who would have the most to gain. Arrogance can be a thin veil protecting a lack of confidence or low self-esteem but it can stand as a real obstacle to progress.

In conclusion, although champions do not share a common personality type they *do* have some characteristics that not only put them at the top but keep them there. One is very basic but probably the most critical – an unswerving capacity to keep moving onwards on their journey. This idea is a key theme of *Pure Sport*. Put another way, whatever has been achieved is never quite enough, there's always more. One of the greatest tennis players of all time, Billie Jean King, recently encapsulated this philosophy during a BBC radio interview, 'It's really important to keep developing your game . . . I didn't think about winning . . . I just think children and young people should realise we all have a different journey, you get there at a different time and keep developing your game'.[8]

A related characteristic is the capacity to cope with pressure and to rebound from failure, allied with a determination to persist in the face of adversity.[9] Even the very best can be beaten and when they are, it is how they come back that matters most. In the famous words of Vince Lombardi, legendary coach of the Green Bay Packers American football team, 'It's not whether you get knocked down, it's whether you get back up.'

Indeed, most top athletes would admit that it is not their triumphs but their adversities (and how they overcame them) that really made them what they are today.

Staying hungry

A related characteristic is hunger – but not a craving for food! What we're referring to is a unique kind of hunger that never goes away – a hunger for improvement. When managed with care this hunger fuels continued success – but it must be managed.

In 2018 Jonathan Rea was crowned World Superbike Champion for the fourth successive year. What does Jonathan see as one key factor to explain his success? Simple, it was having a family:

> I can imagine it being every team manager's worst nightmare when an athlete says: "I'm going to have a kid." But having a family has really helped me. My wife Tatia and my two sons Jake and Tyler give me the distraction to get away from the stresses and strains of racing. It has really changed me for the better . . . I was coming from a really strict mindset, over-analysing and over-training and I was in a bad place. When you have kids, you don't have time. You have to set time aside to do your structured training. It made me less edgy as an athlete – more relaxed.[10]

Following from Jonathan's words, here is one additional piece of advice – learn how to reflect honestly on defeat but never forget how to celebrate your successes. The celebration has to be an integral part of the performance and without due acknowledgement of a job well done then the journey can quickly become less enjoyable and sustainable.

This hunger is like carrying a chip on your shoulder – but remember, you are trying to travel light. As a renowned Gaelic football player and coach once remarked, a chip on the shoulder is plenty – but there's no need for the whole spud! For example, because reality never quite matches up to our expectation then there is the potential for disenchantment, even sulking, and thereby losing motivation. Some of the most highly paid professional sportspeople have shown themselves to be guilty of this crime, not rising to the challenges posed by adversity but instead retreating into a grumpy world of blame and self-recrimination.

In all these cases the key to your journey has to be balance – keeping the edge or chip but maintaining a balance. It is often said that an athlete never truly matures and gains a sense of perspective that allows sport to be given its proper place until he or she has faced true adversity. As one example, Jack Nicklaus, probably the greatest tournament golfer of all time, did not win a major until his father passed away.

Setting off

Many young people set out on their sporting journey because they just happen to be good at sport but without any consideration of the route ahead. As time goes by, their ability may be recognised – and what happens next can be just as predictable. Their talent pulls them down a path and into a competitive system that can take on a momentum of its own. In the process an activity that was once fun and enjoyable may soon start to feel heavy and workmanlike. Sheer drudgery. The burdens of expectation rise as the level of competition increases until eventually the lightness of youth becomes buried under the weight of a sporting career.

Witness the language now used by so many Olympians in the wake of their medal success. It is no longer words such as joy, delight or elation. Instead the modern rhetoric is of hard work and sacrifice, almost as though they have given up their lives in pursuit of a medal. In light of so many recent high profile cases where athletes have described the costs and traumas attached to pursuing their sporting dreams it is no surprise that UK Sport and the English Institute of Sport (EIS) have recently decided to invest in support systems to help top British athletes deal with mental health issues.[11] Likewise, many countries are now introducing strategies and procedures to make sure that sport continues to play a positive role in athlete well-being, from the grassroots upwards.

Young people in sport can become the victims of their own success, not only troubled by personal anxieties and ambitions but also by the collective dreams of those who also live in hope of success. These are not always the Svengalis of sporting fiction or the reviled *pushy parents*. Such people exist, and believe us, they can be scary – but fortunately they are in the minority.

More often supporters are sincere, well-meaning and highly motivated parents, teachers, coaches and relatives who want no more than the best for those that they care deeply for. Sadly, despite these best intentions, their hopes and aspirations can spell a recipe for disaster and disappointment. The high drop-out rates from many sports bear witness to the damage that can be inflicted, and the careful nurturing that is required to sustain interest and enthusiasm through the teenage years.

As one example, all too often promising careers in sport have been nipped in the bud because of an ill-timed comment to the effect that the person does or doesn't 'have it'. Labels stick ('She's a natural'; 'He doesn't have the bottle') and once applied the labels can be hard to peel off. In the Western world especially, we can be far too quick to apply labels or stereotypes. For example, a study looking at why Asian children are so good at maths compared to children in the west found one simple factor, the absence of labels such as, 'He's good at sums', or the opposite, 'She's not mathematically minded'. Asian teachers took it for granted that *all* their pupils had the potential to succeed and so the journey of exploring potential could be undertaken with optimism.[12]

Without knowing it we can quickly consign players to the reject pile by applying labels. In contrast the safest option may be to assume that mental skills and techniques *can* be developed in the same way that physical skills can be sharpened with practice. Yes, of course there are limits to potential, but surely it's better to travel hopefully and explore what those limits may be rather than passively accept your lot?

Changing times

One thing you must recognise that will change during your journey is your unique bundle of motives and expectations. Too often young players and athletes lose the ability to enjoy their chosen sport and play 'heavy' as a consequence. Interestingly, the legendary basketball coach John Wooden (see *Step six*) claimed that a crucial feature of successful sports teams is that they have players who not only work hard but really *love what they do*.[13]

As we'll return to later in the book, the golfer Rory McIlroy went through a difficult time early in his career, on one occasion throwing away an almost unassailable lead in the 2011 US Masters. From the depths of despair, two months later the 21-year-old managed to conjure up an imperious victory in the US Open at Congressional and then went on to win the Shanghai Masters and Hong Kong Open.

What had happened in the meanwhile? One significant event may go some way to explain the transformation. Rory went to Haiti. More specifically, as a UNICEF celebrity ambassador he delayed his preparation for the US Open so as to keep his commitment to visit the shanty towns of Haiti in the aftermath of the earthquake that had devastated the island. His own words at the time reveal the personal impact the visit made on him, 'If you ever hear me complain about a hotel room again, do give me a clout, won't you?'[14]

Why and who?

At some time on their sporting journey, young sportspeople eventually tackle a simple question that may never have even occurred to them in the past but can become an obstacle to progress – why am I doing this? If the answer is not immediately to hand then make no mistake, problems will lie ahead.

Two key questions are critical in laying the mental foundation for a successful trip. Any head time involved in coming up with an answer to either of these questions needs to be examined to find out the source of interference:

> **Q1: Why am I doing this?**
> **Q2: Who am I doing this for?**

The spontaneous answer to the first question has to be . . . for love and enjoyment. There is nothing complicated about playing sport for the pure love or enjoyment of the activity itself but it would be naïve not to recognise that other motives inevitably come along to muddy the waters. It could be that you are doing it for other people, for status, for money, to sustain a lifestyle, for your ego. All these motives may play some role at some time but they often come at a cost, and in turn pure love of the activity can be diminished. This is not necessarily true of other motives such as challenge, competition, fitness or companionship where the sport itself remains paramount and the other motives are fortunate consequences of engaging in that activity – but love or enjoyment must still lie at the heart of the matter.

As to the second question, who, or rather who am I doing this for, again the answer has to be 'pure' or purely for yourself. If along the way this ever fades from view or you feel that others seem to have become more important then there is a need to step back, reappraise and find a way of moving centre stage once more. This does not imply that a row or bust up must ensue but often subtle but effective techniques can be used to move forward.

This is not being selfish, because success benefits everyone, but it is about rediscovering roots and remembering that when everything else is put aside, sport is fun and is inherently selfish – but in the nicest possible way. One of the most successful Irish athletes of modern times, the hurler Henry Shefflin, expressed this sentiment clearly in his own words when he retired from competitive sport in 2015:

> I didn't make any sacrifices. I was just so much enjoying what I was doing. My family members, brothers and sisters and Deirdre (spouse), they made the sacrifices and I'm indebted to them for what they have let me achieve. . . . But they really enjoyed it as well.[15]

At all costs?

Over recent years a variety of factors have conspired together to raise the profile and significance of élite sport, and to increase the pressure to win, whatever the costs. As one example, since 2004 the UK government has adopted a very focused – and some would argue ruthless – policy of only providing funding for those sports and athletes that consistently hit performance targets linked specifically to Olympic medal success. The business model clearly has produced results. At Rio 2016, Team GB won 27 gold medals and finished second in the table – but at what cost? This targeted approach is starting to attract growing opposition, not least among sports that have failed to receive support despite their popular appeal and large participation numbers.[16]

The impact that such policies can have on individual athletes is also starting to be openly questioned, accompanied by a growing disquiet regarding well-being generally among élite sportspeople where the dangers attached to an 'at all costs' approach can be revealed in high levels of depression, burnout and psychological disorders of various kinds.

From the perspective of sport psychology, the 'at all costs' approach sits uneasily alongside a philosophy that is built on intrinsic motivation and the pure enjoyment that goes along with playing a sport that you love.

With this in mind, ironically it is not failure but a preoccupation with *winning* that can often present the biggest obstacles to progress on your sporting journey. Again, Vince Lombardi once supposedly remarked, 'Winning isn't everything, it's the only thing.' Shortly before he passed away in 1970 he openly acknowledged the danger of adopting an *at all costs* mentality. In his own words, 'I wish to hell I'd never said the damned thing. I meant the effort, I meant having a goal. I sure as hell didn't mean for people to crush human values and morality.'[17]

In some respects this is a sad epitaph for such a great man but it is also an honest acknowledgement that a healthy sense of perspective on winning is necessary. Put simply, winning *does* matter – but not to the exclusion of all else. Equally, sport is important – but so are many others things in life. The Liverpool FC manager Bill Shankly once quipped, 'Some people think football is a matter of life and death. I assure you, it's much more serious than that.' He was wrong.

Show me the money

Especially in the modern world of sport, one of the inevitable side-effects of being successful can be the material benefits and celebrity status this brings. In sport, money can be the root of many evils, and the storyline is not new. The Ancient Greek Games eventually lost their appeal and integrity primarily because of professionalism and money. According to a noted historian it was a combination of the two that promoted the message, 'At all costs avoid losing'[18], and when winner takes all then fear of failure becomes a burden that even the most hardy can find hard to shoulder.

Turning to the present day, the greatest darts player of all time, Phil 'The Power' Taylor, went through an uncharacteristically lean spell midway through his own sporting journey. Despite having engaged the services of a sport psychologist he was finding it difficult to rekindle his enthusiasm and his famed killer instinct. His new manager, Barry Hearn, had the wit to recognise that his newfound wealth was interfering with what he did best, play darts, and his solution was simple yet ingenious. After every tournament he told Phil to lodge the cheque in the bank on a Monday and then forget about it. In other words, go back to basics or 'Think poor'.[19] In Phil's own words:

> I've seen a lot of sports people over the years – including dart players – where the money has come into it and ruined their careers. Yes, I've made a bit of money but it doesn't make a scrap of difference to me. If I won £50m on the Lottery it would just go into the bank and then it would be "just move on to the next tournament."[20]

The rest is history. According to Taylor, the game was what mattered most and the tougher it became, the more he loved it, as the following quote reveals so clearly:

> With darts it's just one against one, it's blow for blow. The only thing I could compare it to is boxing. It's dead exciting. You're reacting to each other, the adrenaline's pumping. You don't feel calm at all. But it's all about being able to win when you're pumped up. People say you don't play the player; I play the player every time.[21]

Money can't be ignored but in the white heat of competition, is it the motive that will drive you to go that extra mile? No. Money can be a happy consequence of doing something well but as a motivator it is problematic, and especially when fairness enters the equation, as we will see later (see *Step five*).

Pacing yourself

Fame and fortune can be hard to manage, as can be achieving too much success too soon. Both Neil Armstrong, the first moonwalker, and Buzz Aldrin, the second, struggled coming back down to earth (literally!) because everything else in life paled against this achievement. As mentioned earlier, sport is littered with examples of young stars who burned brightly but briefly and ultimately failed to go on to realise their undoubted promise, a case of too much too soon, or not being prepared for the long haul.

In reality it takes great foresight to acknowledge the need for support when the journey begins, or the path seems easy. Dealing with failure, by contrast, is more straightforward so long as the individual is shown the way forward. It is at this juncture that good coaches, mentors and teachers really come into their own in nurturing young talent (see *Step six*).

Less dramatically, it could be that earlier, sudden improvements in performance become less pronounced or 'plateau' as a career progresses and when practice no longer seems to reap the same immediate rewards. Once the buzz of discovering potential has quietened and reality slowly creeps in then the person may have to come to terms with the physical limits of his or her potential.

In team sports, this can be less problematic as the older player can continue on a journey to explore the team potential and perhaps find other ways to help support the team or club. However, in individual sports the reality check can be especially hurtful.

Taking a break

Another obstacle that almost every sportsperson will encounter at some stage will be enforced rest or absence through injury, an issue that seems to be increasingly prevalent in élite sport. By way of example, it is estimated that around one third of all professional rugby union players are sidelined through injury at any one time during a season, while in American football the NFL has introduced limits to the amount of contact drills and padded practices that teams can have both during training camps and the regular season.

Where there has been a huge personal investment in a sporting life then the adjustment to either enforced rest or retirement can be traumatic. A number of psychological models based on the grieving process have been developed to help understand this process. In a far more positive vein, it is possible to see a period of enforced absence from sport not as a '*time out*' but as a '*time to*'; for example as a time to develop other skills, including the mental.

A time of injury can be used to return not in shape but in even better shape. For example, when the footballer Roy Keane suffered a career-threatening cruciate knee ligament injury in 1998 he was forced to undertake an arduous programme of rehabilitation. During this physical recovery time, he benefited considerably by working on his upper-body strength in the gym, reducing his alcohol intake and by establishing priorities for the remainder of his playing career. Remarkably, as he acknowledged in his autobiography, 'A bleak period in my professional life had changed me . . . time spent alone helped me figure myself out.'[22]

Keep travelling hopefully

At each stage of your sporting journey, different issues and challenges will emerge that can so easily trip up the unwary. No one is suggesting that this will be an easy road to travel but with a few signposts and clear directions it can be an enjoyable and rewarding experience.

To look forward to this adventure, one of the most important points to keep in mind is that you will be travelling through a constantly changing landscape. For example what worked or motivated you as a teenager will be quite different from what will inspire you later in life. For this reason the orientation at each stage of the journey must be dynamic and responsive but throughout such flux, there will be one constant that should never change – a sense of who you are.

The person who begins this journey won't be quite the same as the one who ends it but trying to be someone else along the way won't help. Role models have their place – but keep them in their place! We can watch and learn from them. But beyond this, a role model can do more harm than good to our self-esteem – especially when we try (unsuccessfully) to imitate rather than *learn* from the model. Whereas modelling assumes uncritical acceptance, learning involves a more active process of filtering.

In a similar vein certain sports have adopted the stance of *doing what they did* to try to achieve success. That is, identifying a successful team or nation and then attempting to replicate that blueprint, for example by importing coaches or styles of play. Rarely has this strategy yielded long-term results. Instead, a more likely outcome is a team with a confused identity, and a heightened sense of inferiority as the role model remains just beyond their grasp. Cultures cannot be imported. The alternative is far more appealing and realistic – by all means, beg, borrow and steal practical tips but always remain true to yourself.

Stay grounded

As money continues to be poured into sport it is too easy to buy into the idea that resources will always win out, and that success can be bought. With this in mind, many teams and individuals travel to international tournaments as underdogs with no expectation of success because the form book tells them so. Rubbish! As long as that belief persists then the formbook will prevail – but as long as there are those who are driven to tear up the book then sport will continue to surprise and prosper.

In 2009, Leinster approached the final of the European Heineken Cup against Leicester very much as underdogs. In the days leading up to the final, one of us was contacted by the sport psychologist (and former student) working with the Leinster team, looking for words of advice. The reply that was given was simple, keep it simple, summed up in three short phrases – '*No Excuses, No Script, No Respect*'.

In 2011, Leinster again found themselves in the final but this time not as underdogs but as former European champions. This time the advice was even more simple – '*No psychology!*'. To be more precise, what was meant was don't over-analyse, don't over-complicate; just go out there and play as you know you can! And they did, remarkably turning a half-time 22–6 deficit around and eventually winning 33–22!

The underdog label can be used in either a positive or a negative way but from a psychological perspective it has fantastic potential when handled with care. As a negative, it can help maintain the status quo by keeping people in their place. If you let it then the label can provide a ready-made excuse for failure – but only if you let it. From a positive motivational perspective, the underdog mentality, a healthy disrespect for authority, can work wonders so long as it is underpinned by a sufficient level of confidence. This does not have to extend to *will win* – *can win* is plenty!

Can win . . .

It is a common misconception that the more confidence the better in sport. Unfortunately it's not that simple as the consequences of over-confidence can be disastrous, often becoming associated with complacency or even arrogance. At heart, *will win* is fragile as nothing in life is that certain and entirely under our control. *Can win* suggests we have the capability with the right motivation and circumstance, and is far easier to sustain in the longer term. *Can win* is sufficient to provide the drive to give it a go, and the great advantage of this approach is that the burden of expectation is lifted from the shoulders of those who are then allowed to go out and perform.

Many teams and individuals perform the first part of the underdog trick but often fail at the final hurdle when eventually giving in to the prevailing status quo – otherwise known as GLS or *gallant loser syndrome*. For example, a team that finds itself leading against all odds may then decide that the safest option is to defend that lead. In truth, this becomes the riskiest option as play becomes compressed into little more than a practice game of defence and attack. More rarely a team will have the self-belief to know that what took them to that point can take them further, and that an honourable defeat is still a defeat and is not enough. In other words, *when the going gets tough, the tough keep going* or keep doing what took them there in the first place.

Some situations allow the underdog tag to emerge naturally but how can you hope to continue to persuade champions that they are still underdogs? This must be one of the greatest skills of sport management but it is one that certain individuals have honed to perfection, constantly creating the impression that the world out there is against us, including match officials, administrators and the media. Any examples spring to mind?

. . . but dare to lose

Either through such tactics or in other ways, what a good coach or manager is often trying to instil is a mentality that while the journey may be tough, the goal is within grasp (*'can win'*). However it won't happen by chance and, critically, to be able to win you must acknowledge the prospect of losing. In other words, in order to win you have to *dare to lose*. This is not negative thinking but is reality and actually reflects the coming together of two constructs (our need to achieve and our fear of failure) that have long interested applied sport psychologists.

To explain, the psychological literature suggests that our need to achieve (NAch) and our fear of failure (FF) combine to help determine our approach to competition.[23] Both are entirely independent and so combine to produce a variety of profiles. Typically, scores are used to classify people according to one of four types (see the following).

Summary

Winning and losing 1

TYPE 1 – has a **low** interest in winning but a **high** fear of failing. These individuals will often leave jobs unfinished or lose interest. They will avoid true competition or choose to compete against someone they know they will beat.

TYPE 2 – has a **low** interest in winning and a **low** fear of failing.

These people feel indifferent towards competition and would probably wonder why people make such a fuss about winning and losing. 'After all, it's only a game'.

TYPE 3 – has a **high** interest in winning but a **low** fear of failing.

These people love competition, especially where the outcome is uncertain. They are full of energy towards a particular goal and take calculated risks. They love to win but realise that losing is not the end of the world. They are persistent and highly self-motivated.

TYPE 4 – has a **high** interest in winning and a **high** fear of failing.

These individuals also enjoy competitive situations and take personal responsibility for outcomes but failure causes self-doubt and lowers self-confidence. Anxiety over failing often reveals itself in poor sportsmanship, risk aversion, decreased persistence and a superficial air of arrogance. Such individuals often fail to fulfil their potential.

Not surprisingly, Type 3 people often represent the best long-term investment for any sport. Winning is important to them but losing is not the end of the world. Unfortunately the combination of circumstances that draws a young person into a sport, including the part played by significant others, can inadvertently produce not Type 3s but Types 1 or 4. These may then drift towards becoming Type 2s and finally drop-out.

Those with a high fear of failing will often underperform – not through a lack of ability but through inhibition and an unwillingness to take risks. Poor performances then fuel further fear of failure and so create a downward spiral. The bad news is that many young people do not truly enjoy their sport because of this combination. The good news is that this profile can be changed but only if the person is willing to change. Unfortunately Type 4s can also be characterised by arrogance and this complicates matters as listening is often not their strong suit!

These Type 4 individuals will often have remarkable defences that make sure '*nothing sticks*' (i.e. '*Teflon coated*' or '*Slopey shouldered*'), including critical advice or even support. However, if there is a willingness to change then the process involves going right back to the start and re-establishing the primary motives for taking part – for love of the game, enjoyment and, above all, for yourself. This could include deliberately sidelining significant others and placing more and more personal responsibility on the shoulders of the athlete. With these foundations, a more solid and secure basis for long-term growth can then be fostered.

Hate failure, want to achieve

Looking well beyond the research literature to the reality of sport, the interplay between NAch and FF can often be much more complicated than appears at first glance. Somewhat naïvely many sport psychologists still advocate a model profile based on low fear of failure and a high need to achieve (i.e. Type 3s). In reality often this is impossible to attain and particularly when the amount of investment in terms of time and effort has been so great that failure has serious consequences. Indeed many top sportspeople would say that the fear of losing is what continues to give them the edge. Again in the words of Billie Jean King, 'A champion is afraid of losing. Everyone else is afraid of winning.'[24]

Fear can motivate but it can also inhibit and when it does then alternative strategies may be needed. If fear starts to cramp rather than enhance performance it may be a case of working to turn fear from a negative to a positive. And this is where a *hatred of failure* (HF) comes into play. It is entirely positive to *hate* the prospect of failure and all that goes with it – but to be *afraid* of that prospect is an entirely different matter.

In a similar vein, *needing* to achieve implies a natural force or drive that is imposed and outside your control. A healthier term may be really choosing or wanting it, *want to achieve* or WAch. Although 'wanting to' rather than 'needing to' may seem a small shift, it represents a significant move in terms of placing you in charge of what matters.

Tackling defences

Already we have identified a number of external factors that can have an adverse effect on your progress but what of internal or psychological mechanisms that can stand in your way? Very often these natural mechanisms shield us from harm – and especially when we suffer failure or defeat – but sadly this short-term gain can hide a long-term cost by preventing us from learning from our mistakes. Before going any further, try this short questionnaire on the factors to which we attribute our successes and failures in sport.

Ask yourself

Winning and losing 2

Winning

Think about the last time you won a competition and then indicate the extent to which you feel that each of the following was influential on a scale from 1 to 10 where 1 = not true and 10 = entirely true.

1. To what extent do you feel your ability influenced the result?
2. To what extent do you feel the result was due to your good luck?
3. To what extent do you feel the result came down to your opponent playing poorly?
4. To what extent do you feel the result was because you tried hard?

Losing

Now think about the last time you lost and then indicate the extent to which you feel that each of the following was influential.

1. To what extent do you feel your ability influenced the result?
2. To what extent do you feel the result was due to your bad luck?
3. To what extent do you feel the result came down to your opponent playing well?
4. To what extent do you feel the result was because you didn't try hard?

Now compare your scores on each of the four questions if you're like most people you may find that you're more inclined to take credit for success and to come up with excuses for failure. So you should find relatively higher attribution scores for internal factors (Q1 and Q4) under winning than losing, and vice versa for external factors when trying to explain why you lost.

What is more, whether the internal factor is stable (Q1 – ability) or unstable (Q4 – effort) and equally whether the external factors are temporary (Q2 – bad luck) or permanent (Q3 – opponents) will all have an influence on your willingness to keep going.

Whatever pattern emerges, bear in mind that there are certain ways of explaining events that will be more effective and positive than others in the long run. For example, in order for someone to build on success it is often important to change the way they think about performance – to work hard at acknowledging that a good performance was not because of luck or chance but reflected internal factors that are stable (skill) or unstable (effort). Equally, a poor performance should not be excused away but can be reflected on honestly so as to find useful learning points for the way ahead.

Another crucial word that makes its appearance at this point is *control*. The control that the person *believes* that they have over internal and external factors is vital. Almost all competitors will believe that they can control effort but fewer believe that they can control or influence ability. However do remember that this must be an optimistic journey (we'll explore the importance of optimism again in *Step three*) where change is seen as possible, and where quality practice can move us ever closer to perfection. In this way we can nurture a winning mind by drawing on our experiences, both positive and negative. Looking back to the earlier discussion of the four belief types, high achievers or Type 3s will naturally credit their successes to themselves and their ability, and will deal with failures in various ways (e.g. by dealing with setbacks through increased effort and practice).

On the one hand there may be occasions where you need to put your hand up and acknowledge your failings in order to move forward. On the other hand, when this is taken too far, high achievers can sometimes start to agonise over every mistake and failure, and will believe there is nothing they can do to change the situation. What is more, while high achievers will explain success with reference to stable factors, low achievers will often talk about temporary factors beyond their control when explaining success, and so believe that the performance can never be repeated.

Each attribution style (or way of explaining things) then becomes self-fulfilling, generating either a success circle for high achievers or a vicious circle of failure for low achievers. By attributing their success to internal factors, high achievers will experience more personal pride in their success and so seek out achievement situations. They will persist and try harder when the going gets tough whereas low achievers do not attribute success internally and so become less motivated over time.

For any coach, two key lessons can be extracted from this work. First, from a psychological perspective, the coach's task should be to instil the belief that success relates to effort and ability (internal causes), and that athletes are capable of once more attaining the highest level of skill that they have shown in the past. Second, and equally importantly, strategies for dealing with failure must resist the temptation to make excuses and instead, find positive paths forward.

Knowing yourself

So, we can explain away our successes and failures in ways that are not always productive but forewarned is forearmed and this idea reinforces a key component of your journey – the capacity to be honest and self-reflective. You must strive to eliminate the idea that luck or fate is guiding you and instead explore ways that you can take control of the way ahead, reflecting candidly on previous performances, and especially the 'head' that was carried into those occasions.

This reflection is used to draft a tried and trusted formula for your mental preparation. Techniques including biofeedback (e.g. pulse rate) and mental training (e.g. thought stopping, imagery) can then be used to hit your *zone* (or peak performance state) repeatedly, and stay there. During play itself, other techniques can be employed to achieve two primary aims – to keep your head in the present (not dwelling on past mistakes; not waiting for the end), and to create an environment where thinking does not interfere with doing.

Strangely, this means that on your sporting travels you will need to know not only when to think but also, just as critically, when *not* to think (see also *Step three*). Too often all those countless hours of practice to make the difficult seem natural can be lost when thought interferes, a phenomenon known as *paralysis by analysis*. Losing confidence often refers to no more than the times when the spontaneous has become thoughtful, and stopping those thoughts is a vital skill – but not a difficult one to develop.

The foundation lies in sequencing and so preventing the contamination of one stage by another. Somewhat crudely, these stages can be summarised in three phrases:

> **A: Feck it**
> **B: Do it**
> **C: Think about it**

A. **'Feck it'** refers to that balanced state of mind where the player performs in an unfettered way, knowing that all the hard work and preparation has been done and the primary task now is to play without doubts, worries or expectation – in other words, to give it your best shot.

B. **'Do it'** involves making sure that the clock is never turned back during play itself, so you don't revert to being a novice by thinking about what should be happening spontaneously – or by reflecting on what has happened (especially mistakes). This will only occur if analysis is not allowed to interfere with action. If it does appear, it should appear at the right time, for example during breaks in play. One useful trick to remind yourself that analysis must begin and end is to draw a line on the back of your hand before you play – the line signifying that whatever has happened is past so quite literally you are drawing the line! Or if you are inclined to start taking it all too seriously, why not try a curved or smiley line, to remind you not to take yourself too seriously – and that you have permission to smile at yourself, if necessary!

C. **'Think about it'** is actually the most important phase, for without this one, the other two are impossible. However, depending on the sport in question, there may be a lot, little or maybe even no time for reflection during play itself. Whatever time there is should be used carefully but the most important thinking time should take place almost immediately afterwards, and well before others have an opportunity to comment or judge you. That is the time for a systematic assessment of what went well, what went less well and what must be worked on before the next time. This can then be used as a reference point for discussions with others on your performance and what this means for future preparation.

Psychologists often describe their work in terms of three letters, A, B and C. A or *affect* concerns emotion, B is *behaviour* and C is *cognition*. What this simple three-phase strategy actually achieves is a framework for coordinating and prioritising these three phases in order to produce optimal performance. That is, (A) emotionally the individual must be right when entering competition, ready to meet the challenge but not overwhelmed; (B) during competition, behaviour should be pre-eminent, with cognition or emotion held firmly in check; (C) afterwards is the time for rational thought (cognition), to reflect and analyse and hence provide the basis for future action. In this way the winning mind harnesses A, B and C in that order so as to produce the goods.

Balancing the Cs

As more pieces of the jigsaw start to fit into place, a clearer picture of what is needed on your journey should be starting to emerge. This is not about trying to make you someone that you are not. After all, the core is still you, but armed with a clear sense of purpose, an honest acknowledgement of who you are and who you can be, and so making your sporting journey fascinating around every bend in the road.

As we have mentioned repeatedly, *balance* remains critical throughout your journey. This balance includes four psychological constructs that can help tie together so many of the themes already introduced and that build your mental toughness. A successful athlete will continuously monitor these to ensure that they are acting in concert to make the journey that much easier.

In the past perhaps too much emphasis was placed on only one C, *confidence*, when in fact *commitment* and *control* are just as important.

Too much confidence can be as dangerous as too little because it may foster complacency or cockiness which in turn will lower commitment and control. Too little can have the opposite effect; likewise with commitment. Too much and there is a danger of losing control which will adversely impact on confidence. Too little and the performance will lack passion. In this way too much or too little of any one of the Cs means the mix will be unhealthy; keep them all in harmony and you have a well-balanced athlete who will continue to feel good about what needs to be done and how to go about doing it.

Challenge represents the fourth and encompassing C, defining the overall mental approach underpinning your journey. Each step on this path should be seen as an interesting test of how far you have come and where else you choose to go. At each stage there should still be that buzz of anticipation because the future is uncertain and the end of the journey is unknown.

In this environment, *change* is the only constant as you continue to explore new challenges. And what about those who stand in your way, your opponents? One way to look at them is as interesting obstacles to your progress, obstacles that must be dealt with not according to reputation but according to the practical ways in which they prevent you moving onwards and upwards.

Ending?

At the far end of your sporting career may lurk many mental pitfalls. As for retirement itself, the pain of sudden loss can be intense and especially when the person's sense of identity has been deeply rooted in their sport. Instead, when the time is ripe there can be opportunities to see how that energy and expertise can be reinvested – but timing here is critical. Too soon and the rawness of loss may carry emotional baggage that interferes with rational decision making. Too late and the sense of identity may have reformed around alternative activities.

In many professional sports the end can be sudden and brutal as age takes its toll. To the outsider the fall from grace can appear dramatic. From the inside it is rare that signals have not been picked up that the clock is running down. While denial may cloud judgement, there is usually a moment when a choice has to be made – do I jump or should I wait to be pushed? Research has considered the consequences for those who have not made the professional grade in several sports, including American football, basketball, baseball and soccer. Interestingly, the findings show that being released from a contract is not always as traumatic as may be imagined, and most players eventually find a level that is appropriate to that stage of their career.

Coaches and managers must also deal with the end and, once more, timing is all. In a psychological profiling session we carried out with coaches a few years ago one of the most critical characteristics that emerged was *knowing when to walk* (see *Step six*). In many sports, short-term goals dictate that a coach or manager must produce quick results and when these don't appear then room for manoeuvre can become cramped. Reading the runes in these circumstances can ensure departure is planned and dignified – rather than rushed and imposed.

Off you go!

So, to summarise, what do you need to start your sporting journey? Forget about a set of ingredients that are magically plugged into your head to make you walk, talk and think like a champion. There is no magic bullet. Instead, think about your journey as an interesting expedition to explore new worlds and meet new challenges along the way. As with any expedition, when you begin you will need help to prepare and equip yourself for what lies ahead. As time goes by, instead of taking on more baggage, and guides, your aim should be to learn from your successes and failures, and so lose these burdens and travel lighter and lighter, thereby having the chance to enjoy the scenery around every turn on the road.

Having set the scene, the remaining steps in *Pure Sport* should now go on to help equip you with the right skills and techniques for the journey ahead. Meeting the challenges along the way won't always be easy but then that's what will make the journey interesting and most importantly, enjoyable. With all this in mind, let's move on.

Overcoming obstacles

In this section, we look at a few common problems that those journeying through sport can encounter. We have tried to offer not only a diagnosis of what these obstacles are but, more importantly, tips on how to overcome them.

'I've lost confidence'

From our experience, saying that you've lost your confidence is often a catch-all expression for lots of underlying issues that reveal themselves in underperformance. In fact, it is probably the most common problem that sport psychologists are asked to deal with.

In practice, the statement 'I've lost confidence' usually opens up wider discussion of many issues where the mind has started to impose itself unduly over action, and then performance has suffered. For example, if things have not been going well for you then you may start over-analysing and in the process, digging an even deeper hole (i.e. paralysis by analysis).

At one level, 'confidence' is easy to define. Put simply, it's the *belief* that you can play a certain shot or achieve a certain goal – no matter what. Confident players think they can do it – no matter what. But at a deeper level, confidence is complex. Like any belief, it is shaped by circumstances and so can change. For example, few people are equally confident across all skills. If you're a golfer, you may be more confident with your driver than your wedge. Or if you're a baseliner in tennis, you're likely to be more confident at the back of the court than at the net. Clearly, the fact that confidence is specific to a skill and a situation means that to improve it then you have to *deliberately* work harder on aspects of your game that you least enjoy or want to think about.

A perceived lack of confidence can be the end-product of a process that involves many issues we have spotlighted throughout *Pure Sport*, for example measuring your performance solely by results. It is important that you never fall into the trap of seeing a lack of form as a confidence issue set apart from everything else. Instead, try to develop a more objective and scientific evaluation of your performance to identify the reasons why your form has dipped. This habit of disciplined reflection will help you go back to basics, to identify strengths as well as weaknesses and then use this foundation to develop a programme of rehabilitation, and so gradually re-establish your form.

Speaking of strengths, you may need to remind yourself of your special skills or 'weapons' from time to time, and especially if you have a tendency to judge yourself harshly. These skills are usually ones that you enjoy performing and are most confident about – and they establish a solid platform for the rest of your game.

And remember, you aren't as good as your last game but you are potentially at least as good as your best ever game. Talent never goes away – but it can be mislaid. If your form seems to have slipped, try not to burden yourself with high expectations of making amends by a flawless performance but instead set more realistic goals within a reasonable and attainable timescale. For example, if you're a tennis player whose confidence has dropped because you haven't won for a while, it might be helpful to set yourself a short-term performance target in your next game, such as achieving a certain percentage accuracy of first serves.

Also remember that too much confidence can be as danger-ous as too little. There may be times when everything comes together but a more realistic expectation is *'repeatable good per-formance'* (RGP), adjusting the bar as you progress. Successfully balancing the three Cs (confidence, commitment and control), and learning to enjoy the *challenges* of competition will provide a much more solid foundation for success than overblown con-fidence, best summed up not as a *'will* win' mentality but a *'can* win' mentality.

'I never play well when * * * * * is watching; I'll never be as good as * * * * *'

These statements are related and often suggest that the individual has placed too great an emphasis on *external* reference points or the feelings of others when judging his or her own performance. The expressions indicate thinking that is burdened by a high fear of failure. The solution is straightforward but can take time – to make the athlete more self-contained and self-evaluative. For example, if someone is constantly looking for ego-stroking by others then deliberately put in place performance evaluation pro-cedures that he or she must complete immediately after compe-tition (see *Step four*). In this way, the individual will eventually come to rely more on personal judgements than those of others.

At the same time, he or she will develop a stronger and more comfortable sense of self-identity, and reference to role models should become less important. This can often be a problem during adolescence, at a time when the person may be looking for reassurance from 'significant' others. And the answer is easy – make them less significant!

'I'm finding it hard to come back from injury'

This is a familiar issue for many athletes, and especially when the injury is sudden or interrupts a run of good form. The Irish rugby player Paul O'Connell returned from the British Lions rugby tour to New Zealand in 2005 knowing that he faced surgery and a period of enforced rest. He also had the honesty to recognise that he hadn't played to his potential on tour. In common with the footballer Roy Keane (mentioned earlier in *Taking a break*), Paul's solution was simple. He determined that he would return from injury not just as good as when he left but even better. This is a good example of the type of 'personal best' approach that motivates winners in sport. He then decided to use the enforced 'time out' to consider how he could improve as a player, and left no stone unturned in the process. So instead of the injury time being a frustrating enforced absence from the game, he structured it with a goal in mind – to come back even stronger, which he did.

In contact sports, awareness of an injury can inhibit play. To overcome this heightened monitoring it can be helpful to concentrate attention on highly structured short-term performance goals. In this way, one's attention is diverted from the dominant thought, 'How does it feel?' to the more helpful question, 'How did I play?' By way of example, a previous shoulder injury in rugby may dominate thoughts going into a game and especially around tackling. Replace these general anxieties with very focused performance targets, even down to the mechanics of the tackle itself and including body position and contact area.

Notes

1. Cox, D. (2018). The science wars behind football's penalty shoot-outs. *Al Jazeera* (Science & Technology), 8 July. www.aljazeera.com/indepth/features/science-wars-football-penalty-shootouts-180708095102320.html
2. Psychology Research and References. Home advantage. http://psychology.iresearchnet.com/sports-psychology/team-building/home-advantage/
3. Quasem, H. (2006). Murray shrink kicks up a stink; EXCLUSIVE Top doc hits ace with free book Scot lobs straight into bucket Writer warns him to grow up. http://tinyurl.com/d7nh7h3
4. Mitchell, K. (2012). Coach Ivan Lendl tells Andy Murray to have fun in US Open final. *The Guardian* (Sport), 8 September. http://tinyurl.com/c9m6oc2
5. White, J. (2002). A potter's tale: Any colour will do. *The Guardian*, 20 April, pp. 10–11.
6. Mavericks, C. (2018). Francesco Molinari part 2. *dair Magazine*, 3 July. https://dairmagazine.com/francesco-part-two/
7. Cornell, R. (n.d.). Exercise addiction. ProjectKnow. www.projectknow.com/research/exercise-addiction/
8. BBC Radio 4 Desert Island Discs, 20 June 2018.
9. Sheard, M. (2009). *Mental Toughness: The Mindset Behind Sporting Achievement*. London: Routledge.
10. Rostance, T. (2018). Jonathan Rea: World Superbike champion on how to be a winner in sport. *BBC* (Sport), 16 October. www.bbc.co.uk/sport/motorsport/45666511
11. World Mental Health Day: New plan to help British Olympic and Paralympic athletes. *BBC* (Sport), 10 October. www.bbc.co.uk/sport/olympics/45803592
12. Chen, C., & Stevenson, H. W. (1995). Motivation and mathematics achievement: A comparative study of Asian-American, Caucasian-American, and East Asian High School students. *Child Development*, 66, 1215–1234.
13. Wooden, J. (with S. Jamison) (1997). *Wooden: A Lifetime of Observations and Reflections On and Off the Court*. Lincolnwood, IL: Contemporary Books.
14. Lawrenson, D. (2011). McIlroy given a new focus following UNICEF visit to earthquake-ravaged Haiti. *MailOnline*, 15 June (updated). http://tinyurl.com/ccfm899
15. Henry Shefflin: The next chapter. YouTube, 31 March 2015. https://m.youtube.com/watch?v=n4mg3V1nfJI
16. MacInnes, P. (2018). UK Sport urged to change funding model for Olympics and Paralympics. *The Guardian*, 14 June. www.theguardian.com/sport/2018/jun/14/uk-sport-change-funding-olympic-paralympic-games
17. Cited in Reinharz, P., & Anderson, B. (2000). Bring back sportsmanship. *City Journal* (Spring). Retrieved from http://is.gd/RbOmrN
18. Harris, H. A. (1964). *Greek Athletes and Athletics*. Westport, CA: Greenwood Press.

19. Ronay, B. (2008). Interview: Absolute Power. *The Guardian* (Sport), 25 September. http://tinyurl.com/d87oc9e
20. Turnbull, S. (2009). The Power keeps his eye on the glory. *Independent*, 13 December. http://is.gd/lBfK9q
21. Ronay, B. (2008). Interview: Absolute Power. *The Guardian* (Sport), 25 September. http://tinyurl.com/d87oc9e
22. Keane, R. (with Eamon Dunphy). (2002). *Keane: The Autobiography* (p. 181). London: Michael Joseph.
23. See Roberts, G. C. (Ed.). (2001). *Advances in Motivation in Sport and Exercise*. Champaign, IL: Human Kinetics.
24. Billie Jean King Quotes. Brainy Quote. http://tinyurl.com/ca5ff2s

2 Your mental kitbag

Whether you're a novice or a world champion, in order to travel your own sporting journey with the greatest chance of success you need to *get your head right* or prepare yourself mentally. To do this properly you need to carry two key skills in your mental kitbag. The first one is how to control your nerves and the second is how to use your imagination – or mental 'sat nav' system – to guide your path to successful performance.

In this chapter, we'll give you some practical tips on each of these skills but, in addition, we'll explore them again when suggesting some possible solutions to common mental preparation problems in sport. Overall, this chapter will show you how to develop the right mental approach for optimal performance on your travels ahead.

'Nerves'

Most of us feel butterflies in our stomach when we embark on a new adventure or go across the line to play competitive sport but all this means is that it really matters to us. And make no mistake, it *has* to matter – otherwise why bother to take part at all? So, feeling nervous is entirely natural. In fact, not experiencing butterflies before a competition could be more significant because it might suggest that you're too 'flat', sluggish or lethargic to do your best. Of course, like most people, you probably don't relish the prospect of being tested in front of others. Unfortunately, that's exactly what happens when we compete in sport. So, competition and nerves usually go hand in hand. But what do we mean by 'nerves'?

'Nerves' means being anxious: feeling tense, having a racing heart-beat, being short of breath and dreading an impending event or situation. But it's important to understand that these symptoms are neither accidental nor pathological. They're not accidental because they are part of your body's *fight or flight* reaction – a primitive warning system that prepares you either to confront an imminent source of danger (fight) or to run away from it (flight). And these symptoms are not pathological either. They don't indicate that you're mentally weak or having a breakdown. All they mean is that you *care* about what you're doing. That's why so many athletes are *glad* to feel a certain amount of nervousness before they compete. For example, Dan Carter, the All Blacks outside-half who is a World Cup winner and three-time international rugby player of the year, used to welcome his nervous symptoms before a match because they told him he was ready, 'I had learnt that they (physical symptoms) just emphasised a "buzz" indicating that I was excited and ready for the game.'[1]

Similarly, tennis star Andy Murray, a Wimbldeon and US Open champion, revealed that, 'I'm happy with nerves. For a sportsperson to go into matches being nervous is good. Having that adrenaline gets your mind focused on the match.'[2]

Nerves and mental health: it's ok not to feel ok sometimes . . . but you need to talk to someone about it

In recent years, many leading athletes have publicly acknowledged their struggles with mental health issues. For example, former swimmer Michael Phelps (the most successful Olympian of all time with 28 medals) talks about his experience of anxiety and depression in a film called *Angst: Raising Awareness Around Anxiety* (produced by IndieFlix in 2017). As he reveals:

> I started talking about the things that I went through, and once I opened up about that and things I had kept inside of me for so

many years, I then found that life was a lot easier . . . I got to the point where I understood that it's okay to not be okay.[3]

If you feel that your anxiety is getting the better of you – especially if it's severe, long-lasting and affecting you both inside and outside sport situations – then it may help to seek professional advice from your doctor or from a suitably qualified and experienced mental health specialist (e.g. a clinical psychologist or a counselling psychologist). Other useful resources are *Manage Your Mind: The Mental Fitness Guide*[4] and websites on mental health in athletes such as www.mind.org.uk/about-us/our-policy-work/sport-physical-activity-and-mental-health/ or www.ncaa.org/sport-science-institute/mental-health.

Where nerves or anxiety become so serious that your health and well-being is at risk then it is important to talk and to seek professional help. However, these clinical matters are generally beyond the scope of our discussions here. Instead we would like to look at positive ways in which you can harness your state of nervousness as part of your routine preparation for effective sporting performance. So let's begin by exploring the construct of anxiety in a bit more detail.

Three things you need to know about anxiety

1. Anxiety can either help or hinder your performance – depending on how you interpret it

Whenever you encounter a threatening situation (one that poses a danger to you either physically or psychologically), your brain primes your body for action by releasing hormones (e.g. adrenaline, norepinephrine) into your bloodstream, thereby increasing your *arousal level*. This surge of arousal puts your body on high alert but this sudden increase in arousal is neither good nor bad in itself. Instead, what really matters is how you *interpret* your arousal before a competition. To explain, whereas top athletes like Dan Carter regard high levels of arousal and butterflies in their stomach as a welcome sign of being appropriately 'psyched up' for a game, novice athletes may interpret exactly the same sensations as signs of mental weakness or imminent disaster. The lesson is clear: it's not the *amount* of arousal that affects your performance, it's the way in which you *label* your arousal that matters. To illustrate this idea, here's an example of how a sprinter learned to 'reframe' (or interpret more constructively) his arousal level before a race.

Case study

Reframing arousal before a race

One of us was once consulted by an international sprinter who complained that pre-race anxiety was beginning to impair his performance in competitive athletics. Specifically, he said that his heart used to beat so fast before a race that he felt that rival athletes might even be able to hear it or see it as they prepared on the blocks. After some observation and analysis of his pre-race routine, we discovered a simple strategy to overcome this problem. We trained the sprinter to interpret his anxiety differently by convincing him to identify his pounding heart as the key in his body's 'ignition' – we trained him to believe that when it starts to beat fast, it simply means that he's now ready and primed for an explosive start.

2. Anxiety affects you at different levels

As we mentioned earlier, anxiety is an unpleasant emotion characterised by feelings of tension and pessimistic thoughts. Research shows that it affects you at three different levels: cognitive (thinking), physical and behavioural. First, at the cognitive level, anxiety triggers worrying and takes your mind off the job at hand (a problem that we shall deal with in *Step three*). It encourages you to think too far ahead, especially about what might go wrong around the next bend in the road. Next, at the physical level, anxiety causes increased perspiration, a pounding heart, rapid shallow breathing and, of course, butterflies in your stomach. Third, anxiety can affect you behaviourally by making you speed up and lose your rhythm. In sport, all three levels of the anxiety experience can occur simultaneously. For example, if you're a golfer on the tee-box of the first hole in the Captain's Prize with lots of people watching you, you may worry about hitting your drive into the water, feel extremely tense and swing too fast.

3. We each have our own zone of optimal arousal

Research on the relationship between anxiety and performance in sport confirms something that many of us know intuitively already – we are all *different* in our preferred pre-competition arousal level. Therefore, the person who is best placed to know your 'zone of optimal arousal' is *yourself.*
  So, what is it?

Finding your zone of optimal arousal

Before considering some techniques that you can use to manage your anxiety, it is worthwhile spending a few moments reflecting on the level of arousal that seems to work best for you.

Self-assessment exercise

Identifying your zone of optimal arousal: comparing good and bad performances

The good time

First of all, think of an occasion (maybe in the last six months) where you feel that you played particularly well in a competition. Now, try to remember exactly what you did in the build-up to this event and how you felt immediately before you went out to play. For example, did you try to get some extra rest beforehand or just stick to your normal routine? On the day of the competition, did you arrive in good time or at the last minute? Do you feel that you had too much time beforehand, not enough . . . or was it just about right? Did you go through any practice routine or warm-up exercises – either at home or at the competition venue – on the big day? Did you talk to others (e.g. your teammates) before the competition or did you make sure that you were on your own? Did you feel lethargic or energised beforehand? How calm were you?

The bad time

Now, think of an occasion where you feel that you performed particularly badly in a competitive event – well below what you had expected. Was there any reason (such as illness or injury) for your disappointing performance? Be honest! Again try to remember all the circumstances leading up to and surrounding the event.

Assessing your zone of optimal arousal

Now think of all the other occasions when you either performed well or badly – and what led up to those performances. You can use all these reflections to start to build a profile of the arousal level that works best for you – not necessarily the one you have always used or even the one that you were comfortable with, but the one that really worked best. Having done this, it may be helpful to assess your pre-match feelings on an imaginary 'stressometer' (where 0 = 'completely calm' and 100 = 'panic stricken'!). The purpose of this exercise is to identify your zone of optimal arousal so that you can keep hitting the same mark on the stressometer time and again, whatever the occasion.

By reflecting on the differences between the way in which you felt before performances that were *successful* and those that turned out to be *unsuccessful*, you can gain important insights into your preferred pre-competition routine and your zone of optimal arousal. This routine could include a number of brief relaxation techniques that can help you to hit the mark and stay in your zone. One such technique is the simple *mindful breathing* exercise in the following box. It's adapted from Williams and Penman (2011)[5] and will give you a headstart by helping you to focus on the present moment (a key principle of mindfulness training) while relaxing.

Try for yourself

Mindful breathing – a one-minute headstart (adapted from Williams and Penman, 2011)

One way to prepare for 'hitting the mark' in your sport is to practise mindful breathing while sitting down in a quiet place before you compete. This exercise takes only a minute but requires a quiet place where you won't be disturbed.

Q1. Sit down in a straight-backed chair with your feet flat on the floor and close your eyes.

Q2. Lower your shoulders gently and place your hands flat on your thighs.

Q3. Focus on your breath as it flows in and out of your body. Notice the different sensations that you experience with every breath in . . . and with every breath out. Notice how slowly and deeply you're breathing. There is no need to do anything else – just observe the regularity of your breathing. In and out. In and out.

Q4. After a while, your mind will wander . . . but that's fine. Your thoughts will come and go like clouds floating across the sky. Don't try to control these thoughts – just observe them as they arise and float away. Keep focusing on your breathing.

Q5. Your mind may soon become as calm as a millpond . . . but if it doesn't, don't worry. Accept whatever happens. And remember, keep focusing on your breathing.

Q6. After a minute, open your eyes again and you will feel refreshed.

Many world-class athletes practise similar mindfulness techniques to enhance their performance. For example, LeBron James, the basketball star, meditates regularly – even on court! In fact, during the 2012 US National Basketball Association (NBA) Playoffs, he famously closed his eyes and meditated briefly during a timeout when playing for the Miami Heat against the Boston Celtics. This exercise helped him to block out the noise, quieten his mind and re-focus during a match which his team eventually won. Although James' behaviour may have seemed strange, it was *his* way of getting his head right – and it worked.

What makes you feel anxious in sport?

As you might expect from such a complex psychological and physical response, nervousness in sport is caused by many factors. Here are three of them.

1. A fear of failure

One reason why athletes become anxious is that they engage in *what if* thinking. They may ask themselves, 'What if I fail? What will my coach or other people think of me?' This fear of losing or of letting oneself or others down is very common among athletes. For example, Victoria Pendleton, a former Olympic gold medallist and world champion cyclist, admitted that the, ' . . . feeling I have let people down is my biggest battle in life . . . and when I do, I feel such a failure.'[6]

A fear of failure not only makes you feel tense but also causes you to look too far ahead – making you focus on a possible negative outcome (what might go wrong) rather than on the *process* required to achieve your goal (what you actually have to do in the competition).

2. Unrealistic expectations: the perils of perfectionism

Perfectionism – or setting impossibly high standards for your performance and judging yourself harshly for failing to achieve them – is likely to trigger anxiety competitive situations. Ask yourself, '*Do I expect to play perfectly or to win all the time?*' If so, perfectionism is placing an intolerable burden on your shoulders and you need to learn not to be too hard on yourself. Interestingly, Ben Hogan, one of the greatest golfers of all time, once said that a good round is when you hit *about three shots* that turn out exactly as you had planned.

To explore the perils of perfectionism, try the following exercise.

Ask yourself

Are you being too hard on yourself?

What are your expectations of yourself when you compete? To answer this question, ask yourself if you have any of the following thoughts before or during a game:

- 'I must perform perfectly every time I compete – I'm ashamed of making mistakes.'
- 'If I/we don't win this match against a weaker opponent/ team, I/we might as well give up.'
- 'I should always set the highest possible standards for myself: it's all or nothing for me.'
- 'If I fail in sport, then I fail as a person – it's that simple.'
- 'If I can't be the best in my sport, what's the point of all that training and practice?'

A common theme in these statements is that they put you under pressure unnecessarily because of the black-and-white thinking that they generate. One way of reducing this self-imposed pressure is to stop being so hard on yourself. Also, try to eliminate words like 'should', 'must' and 'never' from your vocabulary – they'll cause you a lot of pointless bother.

3. A lack of confidence

'Confidence' is a belief in your ability to perform a specific skill (e.g. passing the ball to a team-mate) or to achieve a certain goal (to finish a 10k race) regardless of the prevailing circumstances. In short, it's an 'I can do it' conviction. Unfortunately, a lack of confidence is often associated with high levels of anxiety in competitive situations. This happens because confidence is skill-specific and also situation-specific. So, in order to boost your confidence and reduce your anxiety levels, you need to practise harder. As the great golfer Sam Snead once advised a player who admitted to being afraid of certain shots, 'If you're scared of your 7-iron, go and practise it!'[7]

Having explained the nature and causes of anxiety, let's explore now what we know about how nervousness can actually affect your performance.

How does anxiety affect performance?

Earlier, we suggested that the ability to regulate your level of arousal is a vital mental skill in competitive sport. Not surprisingly, many athletes and coaches use self-regulation techniques either to energise themselves when they feel flat or to lower their arousal levels when they feel too agitated before a match. For example, if you're a weight-lifter or are involved in contact sports, listening to inpsirational music before a competition may psych you up appropriately. By contrast, in precision sports (like golf) where calmness is required, active relaxation techniques (like the mindful breathing exercise we presented earlier) may be preferable. But what happens to your athletic performance when you can't control your anxiety?

Choking under pressure

In sport, *choking* occurs when an athlete's normally expert level of performance deteriorates suddenly and significantly under conditions of perceived pressure. Choking is so widespread among athletes that it has different names depending on the sport in question. For example, it is called the *yips* in golf, *icing* in basketball, *dartitis* in darts and *bottling* in team sports such as football. As you may expect, nervousness has prompted some dramatic sporting collapses. For example, golfer Rory McIlroy, a four-time Major winner, squandered a four-shot lead in the final round of the 2011 US Masters championship in Augusta and ended up shooting an eight over par score of 80 to finish *ten shots* behind the winner, Charl Schwartzel. As McIlroy said at the time, 'I was thinking about what could go right but also thinking about what could go wrong. That is no mental state in which to perform'.[8]

Learning from this mistake, however, McIlroy tried a different mental strategy at the 2011 US Open in Bethesda, Maryland – just two months later. This time, he deliberately switched off between shots by engaging his caddie in conversation about movies or football matches as he walked to the ball. The benefit of *not* thinking too much was instant: 'This means there isn't enough time to think about what might go wrong, for negative thoughts, or doubts to creep into your mind'.[9] Remarkably, McIlroy won the tournament by eight strokes.

What is choking?

Choking involves the sudden deterioration of normally expert skills under pressure. What's intriguing about this state of mind is that it seems to stem from a motivational paradox. Specifically, the more effort you put into your performance when you're extremely anxious, the worse it gets. So, it seems that choking is especially likely when you're anxious . . . and *trying too hard* to perform well.

As choking stems from being anxious, its symptoms are similar to those experienced when you're highly aroused physiologically. They include tense muscles, shaky limbs, rapid heart and pulse rates, shortness of breath, butterflies in the stomach, 'racing' thoughts and feelings of panic. But in addition, choking involves the struggle to complete a stroke or movement that you can normally perform effortlessly. This unpleasant feeling of *paralysis by analysis* (recall this term from *Step one*) is well captured by the renowned former golfer and commentator Peter Alliss:

> I stood over the ball, lining up the putt and suddenly I was gripped by negative thoughts. I couldn't visualise the ball going in. I was frightened of failure and I could barely draw back the putter to make contact with the ball.[10]

A similar experience of choking marred the career of the late Eric Bristow, a five-time world darts champion. For almost a decde he visibly struggled with his action and rhythm in trying to release the dart. Bristow attributed this problem to a 'fear of missing.'[11]

What causes choking?

Choking is best understood as an anxiety-based, concentration lapse rather than a personality weakness. This distinction is important because it suggests that *anyone* can choke under pressure if they pay attention to the *wrong* target – anything which is outside their control or which is irrelevant to the task at hand (see also *Step three*). For example, if nervousness makes you think too much about yourself or the importance of the event in which you're competing, your performance may suffer. Psychologically, what's happening here is that you're *reinvesting*[12] or trying to consciously control skills that are better performed automatically. Research shows that in such circumstances, your skills will probably unravel.

Having explored the symptoms and causes of choking, let's now show you how to cope more generally with pressure situations in sport.

Coping with pressure in sport: a five-point plan

Before we give you practical tips on coping with pressure, we need to distinguish between *pressure situations* and *pressure reactions* in sport. Briefly, whereas pressure situations are difficult circumstances that can be described objectively (e.g. playing in a team that is trailing 1–0 in a match with three minutes left to play), pressure reactions (i.e. how you interpret and respond to the circumstances in question) are largely subjective. But because *pressure* is a *perception* not a fact, you don't have to experience anxiety in pressure situations. In fact, you could look at them as exciting opportunities to test yourself against others. With this idea in mind, here is our five-point plan for coping with pressure situations.

1. Restructure the pressure situation in your mind

You are likely to experience anxiety when there is a discrepancy between what you *think* you can do and what you believe you are *expected* to do (i.e. what you perceive as the demands of the situation). Psychologically, therefore, pressure is a subjective interpretation of certain objective circumstances (the pressure situation). Although you can't change a pressure situation, you *can* change your reaction to it using *restructuring* – a technique that requires you to change the way that you look at a situation. The idea here is that by restructuring a pressure situation in your mind, you can interpret it as a challenge to your abilities rather than as a threat to your well-being. For example, former swimmer Michael Phelps used restructuring to boost his motivation. As he said:

> You can look at pressure in two different ways. It's either going to hurt you or help you. I see it as something that helps me. If there's pressure on me or someone thinks I can't do something, it's going to make me work even harder.[13]

A different kind of restructuring was used by eight-time Olympic champion sprinter Usain Bolt during the 2012 Olympic Games in London. Bothered by self-doubt about his slow starts in races, Bolt revealed that his coach solved the problem by convincing him to, 'stop worrying about the start because the best part of your race is at the end!'[14]

To explore this skill of cognitive restructuring for yourself, try the following exercise.

Try for yourself

Turning pressure into a challenge

This exercise shows you how to use a technique called 'restructuring' to turn any pressure situation into a manageable challenge. To begin, think of a situation that usually makes you feel anxious. Now, describe this by finishing the following sentence:

'I hate the pressure of . . . '
Fill in the missing words with reference to the pressure situation you have experienced. For example, you might write down 'I hate the pressure of taking a short putt when a lot depends on it.'

Now, think of this pressure situation again. This time, however, you have to restructure it in your head so that you think about it differently.

'I love the challenge of . . . '

Please note, you're not allowed to simply repeat what you wrote before. You can't just say 'I love the challenge of taking a short putt when a lot depends on it.' Instead, pick something else to focus on in that pressure situation besides the fear of making mistakes. As we shall see in *Step three*, the secret of maintaining your focus under pressure is to concentrate on something that is specific, relevant and under your own control. Usually, that means concentrating on some aspect of your preparation for the feared situation – you could write 'I love the challenge of keeping my head steady every time I putt – no matter what the score is or who I'm playing against.' Notice how restructuring a situation can make you think differently about it. You no longer see it as something to fear but as something manageable or even exciting – something that challenges your skills.

2. Use physical relaxation techniques

In the heat of competition, athletes tend to speed up their behaviour. This is a direct result of the fight or flight reaction that we discussed earlier in the chapter. If you have experienced this problem, the obvious solution is to make a deliberate effort to slow down and relax whenever tension strikes. Of course, this advice must be tailored to the demands of the particular sport that you're playing. One slow down technique that is used across a range of sports, however, is *centring* (see following exercise). To apply it to rugby union, a hooker could easily introduce centring into the line-out pre-throw routine to ensure there is no tension in the upper body and throwing arm. Here's what centring involves.

Try for yourself

Centring

At any stage during play it may be necessary to stop, assess the situation . . . and take control. Centring enables you to quickly and simply counteract physical tension and its associated loss of control. All it takes is a few seconds to calm yourself down to a point where you can take stock of the situation and direct your concentration in appropriate ways.

1. Stand with your feet shoulder-width apart and your knees slightly bent. Your weight should be evenly balanced between your two feet. The bend in your knees is important and should result in you being able to feel the tension in the muscles of your calves and thighs. This flexing counteracts a natural tendency to lock your knees when you become tense.

2. Now, consciously relax your neck and shoulder muscles. Check this by making slight movements with your head and arms (see that they are loose and relaxed).

3. Your mouth should be open slightly to reduce tension in the jaw muscles.

4. Breathe in from your diaphragm, down to your abdomen. Inhale slowly and, as you do, attend to two cues. First, notice that you extend your stomach as you breathe. Next, consciously maintain relaxation in your chest and shoulders. This helps you avoid allowing your chest to expand and shoulders to rise, thus increasing upper body tension. It also counters a tendency to tense your neck and shoulder muscles.

5. As you breathe out slowly, notice the feelings in your abdomen and your stomach muscles relaxing. Consciously let your knees bend slightly, attending to increased feelings of heaviness as your body presses down towards the ground. The exhalation counteracts the natural lifting associated with breathing in and the body does begin to feel more steady.

6. As you have attended to the relaxing physical cues you have simultaneously stopped focusing on the things that were causing you to lose control. Now you should have recovered enough composure to deal in a constructive way with the situation that you face.

To facilitate centring, some professional tennis players use a relaxation strategy in which they visualise an imaginary area (usually located behind the baseline of a tennis court) which serves as a relaxation zone where they can switch off mentally during breaks in play.

If you feel that you may benefit from relaxation skills, try using the following script. It can be used as a general lifestyle tool or perhaps to create the right environment for a good night's sleep. Closer to competition, it may help you to create the right emotional environment during your pre-competition routine.

Try for yourself

Self-directed relaxation

Lie down on a flat, firm surface.

Close your eyes and adjust your position so you are stretched out making maximum contact with the ground. Raise and lower your head to stretch your neck, making sure your neck is not tilted backwards. Flatten your back and push away with your heels to stretch your legs. Take a deep breath and let it out slowly. Feel the weight of your body on the floor, take another deep breath and let the floor support your full weight. Take a deep breath and slowly breathe out. Think of the word 'relax' then pause. Breathe in deeply . . . breathe out slowly . . . breathe in deeply . . . breathe out slowly.

Now focus all your attention on your head. Feel any tension in your forehead. Just relax the tension in your forehead. Relax . . . (pause). Relax even deeper . . . and deeper . . . and deeper.

Feel any tension in your jaw. Just relax the tension in these muscles. Feel the tension flow away. Breathe in deeply . . . breathe out slowly.

Feel the relaxation in your facial muscles. Relax . . . then pause. Breathe in deeply . . . breathe out slowly (pause). Relax even deeper . . . and deeper . . . and deeper.

Now feel any tension in your arms, forearms and hands. Just relax the muscles in your arms. Relax . . . (pause).

Feel any tension in your hands, fingers or arms, and just relax the tension in these muscles. Feel the tension flow away from your body. Breathe in deeply . . . breathe out slowly.

Feel the relaxation in your arms and hands. Relax . . . (pause). Breathe in deeply . . . breathe out slowly (pause). Relax even deeper . . . and deeper . . . and deeper.

Now focus your attention on your neck and upper back. Feel any tension in the muscles of your neck and upper back. Just relax the tension in these muscles. Relax . . . (pause). See the tension flow out of your body. Breathe in deeply . . . breathe out slowly. Feel the relaxation in these muscles. Relax . . . (pause). Breathe in deeply . . . breathe out slowly (pause). Relax even deeper . . . and deeper.

Remember to keep your facial muscles relaxed. Keep your arms and hand muscles relaxed. And keep your neck and upper back muscles relaxed. Keep all these muscles relaxed. Inhale deeply . . . exhale slowly. Feel the relaxation in all these muscles. Feel the relaxation even deeper . . . and deeper . . . and deeper.

Now feel any tension in your lower back and stomach muscles. Focus all your attention on these muscles and get them to relax. Relax these muscles fully. Feel the tension flow away. Breathe in deeply . . . breathe out slowly. Feel the relaxation in your lower back and stomach muscles. Relax . . . (pause). Breathe in deeply . . . breathe out slowly (pause). Relax even deeper . . . and deeper . . . and deeper.

Now feel any tension in your upper legs, both the front and back. Focus all your attention on these muscles and get them to relax. Relax these muscles fully. Feel the tension flow away. Breathe in deeply . . . breathe out slowly. Feel the relaxation in your upper legs. Relax . . . (pause). Breathe in deeply . . . breathe out slowly (pause). Relax even deeper . . . and deeper . . . and deeper.

Remember to keep your facial muscles relaxed. Keep your lower back and stomach muscles relaxed. And keep your upper leg muscles relaxed – keep all these muscles relaxed. Breathe in deeply . . . breathe out slowly. Feel the relaxation in all these muscles. Feel the relaxation even deeper . . . and deeper . . . and deeper.

Now feel any tension in your lower legs and your feet. Focus all your attention on these muscles and ask them to relax. Relax these muscles fully. Feel the tension flow away. Breathe in deeply . . . breathe out slowly. Feel the relaxation in your lower legs and feet. Relax . . . (pause). Breathe in deeply . . . breathe out slowly (pause). Relax even deeper.

With practice, you can gradually combine the muscle groups together into larger units (e.g. head, neck and arms; torso; lower body) until the whole exercise takes only a few seconds to complete.

3. Use a pre-performance routine

A good way to deal with pressure situations is to use a pre-performance routine (or systematic sequence of thoughts and actions) before you execute self-paced skills like a golf putt or a penalty kick. Routines create a solid platform for consistent performance because they take you, step-by-step, from *thinking* about something to actually *doing* it. By immersing yourself in each part of the sequence – instead of worrying about what might happen in the future – routines help you to focus on the present moment. Also, as routines teach you to focus only on what you can control, they protect you from the unwanted effects of pressure and other distractions. To illustrate a routine in action, a Gaelic footballer we worked with rediscovered his set piece kicking ability by developing a pre-performance routine that he had used in his youth. It involved setting the ball on the ground, glancing at the target, looking at the ball, taking five steps backwards, three to the side, looking at the ball again, looking at the posts – and then singing to himself '*We built this city on rock and roll*' as he ran up to kick the ball over the black spot!

4. Think constructively and encourage yourself

When you are anxious, your *self-talk* (i.e. what you say to yourself silently inside your head) tends to become hostile and sarcastic. Although such frustration is understandable, self-critcism invariably makes the situation worse. So when you're talking to yourself, try to encourage yourself for the effort you've shown or to instruct yourself on what to do next. For example, if you're an anxious table tennis player, you might say to yourself, '*Come on, this point now*' (encouragement) or '*Attack the backhand*' (instruction).

5. Get used to pressure situations by training in them

One of the best ways to develop mental toughness is to practise under simulated pressure situations in training. Put simply, preparing for the worst can help you to do your best. For example, Earl Woods, Tiger's father, used to create distractions (e.g. jingling keys, coughing) in an effort to upset his rhythm as he was learning his swing. According to Tiger, such simulated distractions, 'taught me to be completely aware of my surroundings, while maintaining complete focus on the task at hand.'[15]

Using your imagination

Have you ever *seen* yourself in your mind's eye hitting a great golf shot or *felt* yourself making a perfect pass to a team-mate before a match? If so, you're in good company because many world-class athletes use their imagination to prepare for sporting situations and to rehearse exactly what they want to do in them – a technique called *motor imagery practice* (MIP). For example, footballer Romelu Lukaku, the Manchester United and Belgium striker, says that before games, 'I know what I'm doing. I can see an image clearly like on a camera.'[16]

Mental imagery is the process by which we use our imagination to mimic or simulate experiences (e.g. closing your eyes and *seeing* a blue sky or *feeling* sunshine on your face) that are not happening right now. One type of mental imagery is *motor imagery* – seeing and feeling yourself performing a skill (e.g. kicking a ball in your mind) without making any actual movements. Imagery is a remarkable mental skill because it allows us to create virtual experiences of the world – to mentally simulate things (e.g. movements and situations) that seem real but that aren't actually happening right now. For example, when you've read this sentence, close your eyes and imagine throwing a tennis ball high into the air and catching it again. Here, your brain experienced sensations that *seemed real* even though you didn't physically move your arm. Interestingly, the use of motor imagery before a competition is not a new phenomenon. For example, the late Roger Bannister 'ran' a race in his imagination before becoming the world's first *sub-four-minute miler* in 1954:

> Each night in the week before the race, there came a moment when I saw myself at the starting line. My whole body would grow nervous and tremble. I ran the race over in my mind. Then I would calm myself and sometimes get off to sleep.[17]

On this part of your journey, we'll show you how to use imagery to guide you on the path to repeatable good performance. Research shows that top athletes use imagery to rehearse their skills because it triggers similar brain processes to those that are involved in *actual* performance.

Three things you need to know about mental imagery

1. *Your images vary in vividness, detail and accuracy*

Mental images vary in their vividness (or clarity), detail (amount of information) and accuracy (how closely they resemble the imagined movement or situation). The more realistic your imagery seems, the more it will enhance your performance. To improve your imagery vividness and accuracy skills, pay special attention to an object from your sport (e.g. a golf ball) using all of your senses. For example, what colour is it? Does it have a logo? How heavy is it? Does it feel dimpled or smooth?

2. *Your images vary in controllability*

Images also vary in their *controllability* or the ease with which you can manipulate them in your head. Again, the better your imagery control, the more effective is the imagined action. Here's a test of your controllability skills.

Self-assessment exercise

The basketball test

Imagine holding a bright blue basketball in your hands and then throwing it up into the air. Can you see the arc that it traces as it stops and begins to fall back down? Can you imagine catching this ball and then bouncing it three times on the wooden floor of your room? What sounds does it make? If you found these virtual experiences easy to create, you probably have good imagery control skills.

3. Imagery is a skill that must be practised regularly

Imagery is a mental skill, just like any other one, that must be practised regularly for mastery. Here are some tips on practising your imagery skills.

Self-assessment exercise

Using imagery: seven practical tips

1. **Imagine what you're aiming at – not what you're trying to avoid**

   Make sure to imagine a positive target (something to aim at – like a spot on the fairway, if you're a golfer) rather than a negative one (something that you want to avoid – like a bunker or water hazard) because what you 'see' is what you'll get.

2. **Imagine as many details as possible**

   Make your imagery as detailed, accurate and realistic as possible in order to simulate the movement or situation that you want to rehearse. What are the typical sights, sounds and other experiences involved? Close your eyes and try to re-create them in your imagination.

3. *Imagine specific successful actions rather than vague or general results*

It's usually best to 'see' and 'feel' specific skills (e.g. serving accurately in tennis, putting smoothly in golf) – because you're in control of them – rather than results (e.g. winning; which depends on opponents' behaviour). For example, in bowls, try to picture the shot that *you want to play next* rather than the score that you'd like to have for that end.

4. *Imagine all relevant sensory information*

When creating imaginary experiences, it's usually better to include as much of the relevant sensory information as possible. For example, if you're mentally rehearsing a penalty kick in rugby, you should be able to 'feel' the turf under your feet and the weight of the ball as you place it on the ground. You should also be able to 'hear' the sound of the ball as you strike it and to 'see' its flight as you curl it over the bar and between the posts.

5. *Imagine pace accurately – timing is important*

If you're imagining something that can be timed (e.g. a swimming race), check that its imagined duration corresponds to its actual duration.

6. *Imagine in practice sessions as well as before competitiom*

Try to use imagery in your practice sessions as well as before competition. The more you practise imagery, the more it will improve your skills.

7. *Imagine 'trigger' cues*

Imagine key skills using trigger words or phrases. For example, if you're trying to develop a fluent golf swing, imagine what "slow and easy" feels like.

Getting things in perspective: 'seeing' from different points of view

When you *see* an action or event in your mind's eye, you have a choice between two possible perspectives or virtual vantage points. On the one hand, you could imagine someone (either yourself or someone else) performing this skill as if you were watching a video of this person on a big screen. This approach is called *external imagery* because it involves 'looking' at actions performed outside your body. On the other hand, you could try to simulate what it would feel like to perform the skill yourself – rather than watching someone else do it. In this case, you are using *internal imagery* because you're 'looking' through your own eyes, from inside your body outwards. Let's clarify this distinction using a sporting example. Imagine playing tennis on a very windy day. From an external imagery perspective, you should be able to 'see' yourself struggling with your ball toss before serving. From an internal perpsective, however, you should be able to feel the racket in one hand, the ball in the other hand and the wind in your face as you try to serve. To experience your personal preference for one or other of these perspectives, try the following exercise.

Try for yourself

Internal or external imagery? The clock face test

Many of us have a preference for using either internal or external imagery. To explore this for yourself, ask someone to help you with this fun exercise.

1. With their forefinger, ask the person to draw the two hands of a clock on your forehead, with the clock's hands pointing to either 3 o'clock or 9 o'clock – but they mustn't tell you what they drew.

2. As soon as they're finished, say out loud what you think they drew.

3. If you are correct, then your dominant style may well be external (that is, you are looking from the outside in) but if your dominant style is internal then it is more likely that you get it wrong (you are looking from the inside out and so are more likely to report the mirror image).

Which imagery perspective is better?

Which of these two imagery perspectives is more effective? Unfortunately there is no clear answer to this question for two reasons. First, athletes may switch their perspective from external to internal as they become more proficient in their chosen sport. So it's difficult to disentangle imagery perspective choice from experience level in this field of research. Second, each perspective has its own strengths and weaknesses. For example, the benefit of an external perspective is that it allows you to inspect your actions from different positions, thereby enabling you to *zoom in* on any problematic aspects of your technique. By contrast, the benefit of using an internal imagery perspective is that it enhances the vividness of your imagined action. Also, different sport skills may benefit from mental rehearsal conducted using different imagery perspectives. For example, external imagery may facilitate skills such as gymnastics or rock-climbing where body 'form' or shape is important. On the other hand, internal imagery may be more suitable for skills that depend on perceptual sequencing such as slalom skiing. So, let's now consider how we can apply the concept of imagery perspective to a a specific sport – swmming. This example is adapted from an exercise devised by Tony Morris, Michael Spittle and Anthony Watt.[18]

Self-assessment exercise

External and internal imagery in swimming

In order to explore two different ways of looking at things in your mind's eye, let's imagine that you are a swimmer about to compete in a 100m freestyle race.

External imagery

Imagine standing on the blocks along with the other competitors who are lined up on either side of you. You can see yourself as if you were on a large video screen, looking confident and relaxed. Although the other swimmers are standing to your left and right, your eyes are focused on the water in the pool, which looks blue and inviting. You adjust your cap and goggles and prepare for the starter's command. When you hear 'On your marks!', you bend forward – poised and ready for a powerful start. At the sound of the beep, you take off and dive like an arrow into the pool. You are completely immersed in the water and hear nothing. All you can see is your streamlined shape under the water. You break the surface, kick hard and glide through the pool using strong and powerful strokes. You're aware that the other swimmers are beginning to fall behind as you surge towards the wall. As you reach it, you start the turn. Flipping over, you can see yourself pushing hard against the wall as your body is submerged. The shape of your streamlined body is visible under the surface. As your head breaks the surface again, you can see that you're still in the lead. Looking totally focused, you glide through the water using powerful strokes.

Internal imagery

Imagine standing on the blocks along with the other competitors who are lined up on either side of you. You feel that you are really there. You look around at the other competitors and are fully aware of all the sights and sounds around the pool. You can smell the chlorine at the pool and the water seems inviting. You adjust your cap and goggles until they feel just right and bounce up and down on your toes as you wait for the starter's command. When you hear 'On your marks!', you bend forward slowly and prepare your body for a powerful start. At the sound of the beep, you take off and dive like an arrow into the pool. As soon as you hit the water, your body feels completely immersed. Your body feels streamlined and you kick hard. When you break the surface, you kick hard again and you can feel your powerful strokes helping you to glide through the pool. You're aware that the other swimmers are beginning to fall behind as you surge towards the wall. As you reach it, you start the turn. Flipping over, you can feel yourself pushing hard against the wall as your body is submerged. You start the turn, throwing your legs over your head and pushing your streamlined body tight and hard. As your head breaks the surface, you can see that you're still in the lead. Feeling totally focused, you glide through the water using powerful strokes.

(Based on Morris, T., Spittle, M., & Watt, A. (2005). *Imagery in Sport*. Champaign, Ill: Human Kinetics.)

Now that we've explored what imagery pespectives involve, let's consider how motor imagery practice works.

Motor imagery practice (MIP)

As we explained earlier, motor imagery practice (MIP) involves systematically rehearsing skills in your imagination before actually performing them. For example, here is how you could apply it to golf putting.

Self-assessment exercise

Motor imagery practice: golf putting

The purpose of this exercise is to help you to 'see' and 'feel' your putting stroke in your mind's eye. By learning to imagine this stroke, you can practise it even when you're not playing golf. Please make sure that you are sitting comfortably with your eyes closed and that you will not be disturbed for the next few minutes.

Imagine standing on the green of a particular hole at your local golf course on a bright summer morning. The flag is lying to the side of the green casting a small shadow from the sun and you are all alone. Your ball is lying about a metre from the hole and you are standing comfortably beside it. As you look at the ball, you can see it gleaming in the sunshine and feel the weight of your putter in your hand. You can also feel the springy grass underneath your feet.

Walking slowly up to the ball, you stand behind it and crouch down to assess the situation – noting a slight slope to the left. After a few seconds, you begin to see the best line for your putt and to make absolutely sure, you trace an imaginary white line between the hole and your ball. Slowly, you allow your eyes to gaze back and forth along this white line – back and forth, back and forth. Your target for this line is a slightly yellowish blade of grass which lies about two inches from where your ball lies. You look carefully at this blade of grass to remind you of the line you have chosen.

Then you stand up slowly and approach the ball. Standing directly over the ball, you lower your shoulders, get comfortable and adjust your feet so that you're standing square to your putting line. Your set-up feels nice and relaxed and you breathe out gently – slowly and deliberately. Then, keeping your head still, you take two or three gentle practice swings – feeling your shoulders, arms and putter working together as a solid unit. Feel the smooth follow-through of your practice swing each time. Now, you're ready. So, you glance at the hole one more time, focus on the yellow blade of grass, and prepare to putt. Slowly and gently, you roll the ball down the line.

Now, we'll explain how you can apply MIP to your own sports.

Motor imagery practice (MIP): a three-step process

MIP involves three steps – physical relaxation; creating and replaying your image; and finally, building imaginary rehearsal into your pre-performance routine. Before you begin these steps, however, you must be quite clear and specific about the specific skill or situation that you'd like to rehearse in your mind's eye. Let's start by pausing for a moment to pick a specific skill that you would like to practise in your mind (see the following).

Try for yourself

Motor imagery practice (MP)

The skill which I want to practise is

_____

When did you last perform this skill correctly and what did it feel like?

_____

(*We ask this question so that you will bring to mind a specific and vivid example of yourself performing this skill successfully.*)
Now that we've picked a skill to work on, let's explore the four steps of mental practice.

Step 1: Relax

Physical relaxation can help to free your imagination. That's one of the reasons why you often find yourself daydreaming as you sit comfortably in a bus or train. A useful way to relax your body is through deep breathing – conducted with your *diaphragm* rather than with your chest. Before you begin this exercise, sit down in a quiet place and close your eyes. Now, slowly 'centre' your body by lowering your shoulders gently. Then, gently flap out any tension in your arms and legs. After that, take ten deep breaths, making sure that you're pushing your stomach *out* slowly when you breathe in and pulling your stomach *in* gently when you breathe out. Over time, you can train your body to relax even better by saying the word 'RELAX' to yourself as you breathe deeply. One way of doing this is to say **'RE'** when you breathe **in** – and **'LAX'** as you breathe **out**.

Step 2: Create and rehearse your image

Now that you feel relaxed, you will find it easier to create the skill that you wish to imagine. Close your eyes and imagine the venue where you will be performing this skill. Now try to see yourself doing this skill successfully. Take a few minutes to imagine this scene as vividly as possible – notice details of the sights, sounds and bodily sensations which you are experiencing. Now, 'see' and 'feel' yourself performing the skill smoothly and correctly. Notice how calm and confident you feel as you perform the movements in your mind, over and over again for about two to three minutes.

Step 3: Build imagery into your routine

Combining motor imagery with a pre-performance routine is a technique for improving your concentration. As we explained earlier in this chapter, a pre-performance routine is like the steps of a staircase that takes you from thinking to action.

Overcoming obstacles

In this section, we look at a few common problems that those journeying through sport can encounter. We have tried to offer not only a diagnosis of what these obstacles are but, more importantly, tips on how to overcome them.

'I can't always rise to the big occasion . . . sometimes I feel a bit flat'

There's an old old maxim in sport that says: 'Success comes in *cans* . . . not *can'ts*! So, if you can identify your zone of optimal arousal – that critical point on your personal 'stressometer' which tells you that you're ready to compete – then you CAN play to your full potential, regardless of the occasion. Remember that if you did it before, you can do it again. By reflecting on how you prepared for a previous best performance, you can develop a pre-match routine that allows you to get into the groove every time you compete. For Tiger Woods, a 15-time Major winner to date, a key feature of his preparation for tournaments is just how *unremarkable* it actually is. He knew what worked and so didn't change his routines. Why change a winning formula?

> One of the biggest mistakes any player can make is treating the majors as something special. In terms of preparation, Tiger Woods does not do that. Tiger gets a lot of credit for being able to get his game in its best shape for the biggest four weeks of the season, but the fact is that he warms up for every event as if it is a major. That is his 'secret'.[19]

Important sporting occasions tend to bring to mind a host of 'what ifs' in athletes' thinking. If you are worried about losing a match or are afraid of letting other people down, then you need to switch your focus to a small set of personal performance goals (e.g. 'I'm going to go through my routine no matter what's at stake' or 'I'm going to keep up with play'). Before competition, make sure that you create space to do your own thing and don't be caught up in other people's preparation routines.

'I feel exhausted and burnt out these days . . . I'm just not enjoying my sport any more'

Some athletes find that the stress and relentless training demands of competitive sport drain their enjoyment of the game – causing them to feel exhausted and burnt out. If you can identify with this experience at present, don't despair – there are many ways to 're-charge your batteries'. For example, relaxation techniques and mindfulness training can ease your anxiety and boost your ability to cope with stress. Also, taking a break and talking to an experienced and competent mental health professional (e.g. a counsellor or clinical psychologist) about your feelings may be helpful. Such a person may be able to help you to re-discover the joy of sport and the healthy benefits associated with it. Finally, remember that you are not defined solely by what you do or what you achieve in sport – you are MORE than 'just an athlete'. Sometimes, feeling burnt out is a sign that you need to take a step back to spend some time exploring what you enjoy most in life.

'I find myself thinking quite negatively before games – imagining the worst things that could happen'

As we explained earlier, our imagination is a powerful mental 'sat nav' system that can prepare you for the future and guide you to sporting success. But like any sat nav, it can backfire if it's programmed with unhelpful information. For example, have you ever found it hard to sleep at night because you were worried about missing an early flight the following morning? If so, you know what it's like to be upset by negative thoughts and distressing mental images – even if what you've feared the most may never actually occur. Mark Twain is said to have captured this idea of negative imagery perfectly when he remarked, 'I have been through some terrible things in my life, some of which actually happened!'.

And so, many athletes torture themselves by imagining a host of negative scenarios before they compete – a practice that *hampers* rather then helps their mental preparation. So, if you find your imagination running riot with negativity before a match, try saying "STOP" to yourself and focus instead on what exactly you want to do well. Why punish yourself by imagining what might go wrong? It's much more effective to 'see' and 'feel' yourself performing calmly and confidently in the competition in question. Remember, what you see is what you'll usually get.

'I never seem to be able to reproduce in games what I've shown I'm capable of in practice'

This is a common problem among those who have not developed standard pre-match routines to ensure consistency of approach, or who have not come to terms with the arousal levels that work best for them. Less commonly, this may be because the athlete has lost interest in competition for some reason; where this is the case then it would be important to understand why.

For those who can't translate practice into competition, the starting point must be quantifying or measuring how large the gap is before looking at ways of bridging the gap. It is unlikely this will be achieved overnight but instead will involve a measured process that involves minimising the difference between the two, for example by treating competition as no more than another practice session, or making each practice more like actual competition. This problem may take time and effort to resolve but is not insurmountable.

Notes

1. Wagstaff, C., Neil, R., Mellalieu, S., & Hanton, S. (2011). Key movements in directional research in competitive anxiety. In J. Thatcher, M. Jones, & D. Lavallee (Eds.), *Coping and Emotion in Sport* (2nd ed., pp. 143–166). London: Routledge.
2. Mitchell, K. (2010). Hard regime in gym helps Murray find his feet on clay. *The Guardian* (Sport), 29 April, p. 6.
3. Kennedy, M. (2017). Michael Phelps opens up about struggles with depression and anxiety in new documentary. *The Globe and Mail*, October 11. www.theglobeandmail.com/sports/more-sports/michael-phelps-opens-up-about-struggles-with-depression-and-anxiety-in-new-documentary/article36539695/ **accessed** on 11 September 2018.
4. Butler, G., Grey, N., & Hope, T. (2018). *Manage Your Mind* (3rd ed.). Oxford: Oxford University Press.
5. Williams, M., & Penman, D. (2011). *Mindfulness: A Practical Guide to Finding Peace on a Frantic World*. London: Piatkus.
6. McRae, D. (2011). Victoria Pendleton reveals her doubts, dreams, and disappointments. *The Guardian* (Sport), 29 October, p. 2. www.theguardian.com/sport/2011/oct/28/victoria-pendleton-interview accessed on 11 September 2018.
7. Faldo, N. (2012). *A Swing for Life: Revised and Updated*. New York: Atria Books.
8,9. Syed, M. (2017). Courageous Jana Novotna an example to all. *The Times* (Sport), 21 November, p. 55. www.thetimes.co.uk/article/courageous-jana-novotna-an-example-to-all-gdttghs37 accessed on 11 September 2018.
10. England must find the cure for the spot-kick 'disease'. *The Guardian*, 19 May 2000, p. 35.
11. Haigh, P. (2017). What is dartitis? Affliction explained after Berry van Peer's Grand Slam of Darts trauma. *Metro* (Sport), 13 November. https://metro.co.uk/sport/ accessed on 11 September 2018.
12. Masters, R. S., & Maxwell, J. P. (2008). The theory of reinvestment. *International Review of Sport and Exercise Psychology*, 2, 160–183.

13. Keeping cool with Michael Phelps. *BBC Sport Academy*, 2 May 2007. http://news.bbc.co.uk/sportacademy/hi/sa/swimming/features/new sid_3921000/3921525.stm accessed on 11 September 2018.
14. Bee, P. (2012). The golden rules. *The Sunday Times* (Style), 19 August, pp. 22–23.
15. Benedict, J., & Keteyian, A. (2018). How Tiger's father treated his son as a prisoner of war to toughen him up. *The Times* (Sport), 24 March, p. 17.
16. Hunter, A. (2016). "I can see an image clearly like on a camera. I know what I'm doing". *The Guardian* (Sport), 19 March, p. 6.
17. Bannister, R. (2004). Fear of failure haunted me right to the last second. *The Guardian* (Sport), 1 May, p. 12.
18. Morris, T., Spittle, M., & Watt, A. (2005). *Imagery in Sport*. Champaign, Ill: Human Kinetics.
19. Casey in prime condition for best shot at green jacket. *The Sunday Times* (Sport), 4 April, 2007, p. 2.

STEP 3

Travelling light

The ability to travel light – or shed excess mental baggage – is vital during your journey through sport. For example, consider the case of Pete Sampras, a 14-times grand slam tennis champion, who won Wimbledon in 1999 with an ace on his *second* serve in the final against Andre Agassi. After the match, Sampras was asked what had been going through his mind at that stage. His answer was extraordinary, 'There was absolutely nothing going on in my mind at that time.'[1]

Later, he was more forthcoming about his experience of playing tennis finals. Specifically, he explained that although he was always nervous on the day of a grand slam final, 'Something would happen when I walked on to play. . . . My head would clear out all the other stuff and focus on something incredibly simple.'[2]

This idea of emptying your mind in order to perform well is echoed by other winners in sport. For example, golfer Ben Crenshaw, who won the US Masters tournament twice, explained the mental difference between players who win and those who don't, 'The difference, when there are so many at the same skill level, is an uncluttered mind.'[3]

But how exactly do we declutter our minds in order to focus effectively on the task at hand, especially when adversity strikes? In this chapter, we'll show you how to improve your *concentration* (the ability to focus on what you're doing while ignoring distractions) and increase your *resilience* (the ability to bounce back from adversity) – the mental keys to travelling light. We'll also examine some common problems that arise along the way when setbacks affect our focusing skills.

Concentration: focusing on what you're doing

'*Come on, concentrate!*' Has a coach or team-mate ever shouted this instruction at you during a game? If so, it's unlikely to succeed – for a rather obvious reason. Although a request to *concentrate* may encourage you to try harder, it fails to tell you *exactly* what you should focus on or do. So, asking you to concentrate is not helpful unless the request is linked to a specific action – preferably one that's under your control right now. For example, if a fellow defender in football urges you to 'hold the line', then you know exactly what you have to do. In this case, it's easy to concentrate because your mind can 'lock on' to a specific target action.

But as you've probably discovered by now, it's difficult to *stay focused* for long – mainly because of the way in which our minds work. To explain, the brain system that controls our concentration is called *working memory*. Unfortunately, this system is easily overloaded (e.g. try multiplying 23 by 39 in your head!) and very 'leaky' (e.g. have you ever travelled from one room to another in your house in search of something only to discover that you'd forgotten what you were looking for?). And so, because of these 'hard-wired' limitations in our brain, we can pay attention consciously to *only a tiny fraction* of the vast amount of information that bombards us every day.

On our sporting travels, our ability to focus on the task at hand is challenged by a multitude of possible distractions – whether coming from the world around us (e.g. noise, sudden movements) or from our own thoughts and feelings (e.g. '*I feel nervous: I'm going to make a mess of this shot*'). Yet, despite struggling with excess mental baggage, successful athletes manage to *travel light* . . . by blocking out distractions and focusing effectively on the task at hand. For example, Usain Bolt, a multiple Olympic gold medallist and probably the greatest sprinter of all time, gave this simple advice on how to prepare for a race, 'Don't focus on the guy next to you. He might be very quick out of the blocks, which can make you lose concentration. Stay focused on what you're going to do and run your race at all times.'[4]

The lesson from Bolt is clear – empty your mind of thoughts about your opponent and instead, focus on what *you're* going to do. That's the secret of travelling light. But how can you clear your mind of all its clutter and concentrate fully on the way ahead – while encountering mistakes and setbacks? In this chapter, we're going to explain what concentration is, show you how to handle distractions, and give you some practical tips on focusing effectively in sport. We'll also show you how to learn from your mistakes and setbacks.

Concentration: three things you need to know about your mental spotlight

As we explained earlier, concentration (or *focusing*) means paying attention to the task at hand while ignoring distractions. Psychologically, your concentration beam is a mental spotlight – just like the head-mounted torch that miners, divers and potholers wear when travelling through dark environments. Wherever they shine their torch, their target is illuminated. With this idea in mind, here are three things that you need to know about your mental spotlight.

1. Your spotlight can be either broad or narrow

You can adjust the beam of your mental spotlight to be either broad or narrow. A *broad* focus allows you to absorb lots of information rapidly. For example, before you take a throw-in in football, you quickly check your team-mates' positions. A *narrow* focus ensures that you have only one thing on your mind before you execute a skill. For example, you must decide which side of the goal to aim at before you take a penalty kick. Both types of focus are required at different times in all sports.

2. You can shine your spotlight inwards as well as outwards . . . but you can't 'lose' it

Your concentration beam is different from a head-mounted torch in one crucial way – it can shine *inwards* as well as *outwards*. For example, have you ever realised that you've been reading the same sentence in a book over and over again without any understanding because your mind was 'miles away'? If so, then you have first hand experience of *losing* your concentration. But is it ever really lost? After all, your mental spotlight didn't just disappear – it has to be shining *somewhere*. So, when your concentration lapsed while reading, you *distracted yourself* by allowing a thought or daydream to become the target of your mental spotlight. And so, concentration can never be truly lost – although it can be *diverted* to something (in this case, a thought/daydream) that's irrelevant to the task at hand. That's what Usain Bolt meant when he admitted how easy it is to *lose concentration* by focusing on your opponent in a race. Looking at someone else can divert your focus from what *you* have to do. But remember – you're in control of where you shine your own concentration beam. For example, if you look at your coach for final instructions just before the start of a match, you've chosen an *external* focus of attention at that moment. But when you dwell on your own bodily sensations (e.g. the butterflies in your stomach before kick-off), you have switched to an *internal* focus of attention. Typically, in team sports, an external focus of attention is required when you're trying to read a game, pass to a team-mate or mark an opponent. By contrast, an internal focus is needed when you're going over a game plan in your mind's eye before a match (see also *Step two*).

3. You can have four different types of focus

If we combine the two ideas concerning the *width* (broad or narrow) and *direction* (external or internal) of your concentration beam, you can see that there are four different types of focus – broad external, broad internal, narrow external or narrow internal (see the following).

Summary

The four types of focus

- **A broad external focus**
  This focus is required to read a game or assess a sport situation for relevant information. For example, in football or

hockey, a good midfield player must be able to quickly weigh up the best passing options available to him or her.

- **A narrow external focus**

  This type of focus is necessary whenever an athlete aims for a target. For example, if you're a golfer standing on the tee-box, you need to pick a specific spot on the fairway towards which you're going to drive your ball.

- **A broad internal focus**

  This focus is called upon when you're going through a tactical plan in your head before a forthcoming match.

- **A narrow internal focus**

  This type of focus is required when your mind has to concentrate on a single thought or idea such as your stride or your breathing when running a marathon.

Now that you've learned about the four different types of focus, a practical question arises. Is your current focus *appropriate* for the skill that you're trying to perform? As we explained in *Step two*, thinking too much about the mechanics of a skill can cause it to unravel (paralysis by analysis, a term we introduced in *Step one*). Likewise, shining your spotlight on *yourself* as you perform is not a good idea as it makes you too self-conscious. And focusing on what might happen in the *future* is counter-productive because it encourages you to think too far ahead. So, what's left? The answer is simple: focusing on the task at hand. But to do that effectively, we have to block out distractions.

Distractions

Although distractions come in all shapes and sizes, they can be divided into two main categories based on where they come from – *external* (outside world) or *internal* (inside your own head). External distractions are things (including people, events and situations) in the world around you that divert your concentration beam from its intended target. By contrast, internal distractions are psychological events and experiences (including thoughts, feelings and/or bodily sensations such as pain or fatigue) that upset your focus.

Summary

External distractions	*Internal distractions*
Crowd noise/spectator behaviour	Thinking too far ahead
Certain weather conditions/ playing surface	Dwelling on past mistakes or missed chances
Gamesmanship by opponents	Reflecting on how you are feeling
Overuse of social media	Worrying about other peope's reactions

External distractions

Common external distractions include factors such as spectator behaviour, unfavourable weather conditions, gamesmanship by opponents and overuse of social media. For example, golfer Jordan Spieth, a three-time Major winner, missed the cut at the Phoenix Open in 2018 because a sudden shout from a spectator caused him to miss a make-or-break putt on his final hole. Not surprisingly, this person was subsequently ejected from the tournament. But shouting by opponents can also be distracting. To illustrate, consider an incident that happened during the 2011 US Open tennis final between Samantha Stosur and Serena Williams. Williams had lost the first set and was facing a break point in the first game of the second set when she hit a forehand and shouted, '*Come on!*' before the ball reached Stosur. As this shout was deemed to be a deliberate hindrance by the umpire, Williams forfeited the point and lost the game – and eventually the match. Gamesmanship, or pushing the rules to the limit in order to distract or unsettle your opponent, is widespread in football, cricket, golf, tennis and snooker. For example, at corner-kicks in football, the opposing team's players often stand in front of the goalkeeper to prevent him/her from tracking the flight of the incoming ball. In a subtler vein, athletes often use apparently spontaneous banter to disrupt their opponents' concentration. In cricket, this verbal warfare is known as *sledging*. To illustrate, Shane Warne, one of the greatest bowlers in the history of the game, used to disrupt batsmen's concentration by getting them to think too much about some aspect of their technique. Specifically, he admitted that, 'I'd try and get inside their head a bit, too. Sometimes, I'd just say to someone "You've changed your stance then?" – just to get them thinking, "Have I?".'[5]

Of all the external distractions affecting athletes, perhaps the most recent and least investigated are digital ones – those that stem from excessive use of *social media* or websites and applications (e.g. Facebook, Snapchat, Twitter, Instagram) that enable us to create and share content and to engage in social networking with other users. Perhaps not surprisingly, world-class athletes such as the footballer Cristiano Ronaldo are among the most extensively 'followed' celebrities in the world at present. Unfortunately, following people online or responding to those who follow you, is potentially distracting. To address this problem, many coaches and sports performers have begun to experiment with social media blackouts prior to important competitions. For example, alpine skier Mikaela Shiffrin, a two-time Olympic gold medalist, stopped using Instgram, Twitter and Facebook for two weeks before her success at the 2018 Winter Olympics in order to avoid distractions, 'If I can't see it then I don't know what people are saying and it really feels like it is just me out there, and then I can just ski for myself.'[6]

If you would like to avoid digital distractions, here are some pratical tips:

Self-assessment exercise

Handling social media: reducing digital distractions

How often do you check your smartphone each day? Are you obsessed with finding out what your friends are up to from hour to hour? Is your reliance on social media getting in the way of your training or work? If you answered 'yes' to these questions, then you may need some practical tips on reducing digital distractons in your life.

- **Take regular 'tech checks' . . . but set a timer!**

  If you're finding it hard to resist digital distractions, plan short (three minutes) but regular 'tech checks' where you allow yourself to check your emails or newsfeeds. Use a timer to make sure that you stick to your plan.

- **Turn off notifications**

  To avoid the sound of 'bleeps' and 'pings' from your phone, tablet or computer, turn off all notifications from electronic devices when you want to work or train.

- **Change your preference settings**

  Change the frequency with which you're updated when one of your 'friends' uploads something new.

- **Out of sight is out of mind**

  Put your phone or other electronic device out of sight – and out of hearing. What you can't see or hear is not likely to distract you.

- **Edit your apps**

  Do you really need all the apps on your phone?

- **Cut down your social media use**

  You don't have to be active on all social media sites. Which ones can you do without?

- **Visit friends or go for a walk with them**

  If you really feel the need to connect with other people, why not visit them in person or arrange to go for a walk with them for a catch-up conversation?

Internal distractions

Internal distractions are thoughts, emotions (e.g. anger) and/or bodily sensations (e.g. pain, fatigue) that prevent you from concentrating fully on the job at hand. One such self-generated distraction is thinking too far ahead – wondering about what might happen in the future rather than focusing on what you have to do right now. For example, after golfer Rory McIlroy had 'choked' (see *Step two*) in his final round at the 2011 US Masters, he revealed that he had been distracted by his own thinking on the course, 'I spent the last five holes thinking about what I was going to say. That is why my interview afterwards was so good. I spent about two hours thinking about it!'[7]

Another common internal distraction is anger. Although it may give you a temporary surge of energy, anger damages your performance in two ways. First, it blinds you to other ways of seeing things. For example, if you've been fouled by an opponent you may miss the opportunity to take a quick free kick because you're intent on seeking retaliation. Second, anger wastes energy and prevents you from going beyond the trigger (e.g. an unfavourable refereeing decision) that activated it originally. Acknowledging this point, former tennis champion John McEnroe admits in his book *But Seriously* that he wasted a lot of energy getting angry about line-calls during his tennis career – energy which should have been channelled into his performance. Supporting this idea, there are many fascinating examples of athletes whose performance actually *improved* when they learned to curb their temper. Perhaps most remarkably, consider the case of Bjorn Borg, the 11-time grand slam tennis title winner. Although renowned for his calm temperament, Borg had been an extremely angry and volatile player in his early years:

> When I was twelve, I behaved badly on court, swearing, cheating, throwing rackets – so my club suspended me for six months. When I came back, I didn't open my mouth . . . I felt that I played my best tennis being focused.[8]

Clearly, Borg wasn't always as cool as the iceberg that he became in later years! The lesson here is that with proper self-control, *hot anger* can be channeled into *cool concentration*. More generally, as you might expect, winners in sport tend to have an emotional profile that is characterised by relatively low levels of anger when compared with less successful athletes. This is known as the *iceberg profile*[9] because negative mood scores are all *below* the average (or water-line), while the score for vigour or physical intensity is *above* that line.

In order to help you to improve your composure in the heat of competition, here are some practical tips for managing your anger:

Try for yourself

Anger management – a five-step process

1. **Identify the warning signs**

   The first step in anger management is to recognise the bodily signals (e.g. racing heart, angry thoughts) indicating that a 'red mist' is about to descend on you.

2. **Reframe your personal anger triggers**

   Practise ways of reframing (looking at or interpreting differently – see also *Step two*) the situations that normally trigger your anger. For example, if you've been the victim of a nasty tackle from an opponent, you could say to yourself 'They can't handle me – that's why they had to foul me: I'll show them!'.

3. **Press the 'pause' button and breathe deeply**

   Once you feel yourself losing control of your angry feelings, press an imaginary pause button in your head. This will give you time to cool down and use relaxation techniques – like breathing deeply or imagining a calm place – before stepping away from the situation.

4. **Walk away**

   It always helps to walk away from trouble. Implementing this idea, Tiger Woods devised a 'ten-yard line' for himself

> whereby he ensured that all the anger that he had felt after a poor shot would be dissipated by the time he'd walked ten yards from the spot where he'd hit it.
>
> **5. Seek help from others**
>
>   If persistent anger is distracting you and getting you or your team into trouble, then you may need to seek professional advice from a suitably qualified and experienced psychologist or counsellor.

Exploring your distractions

In this section let's explore the distractions that you experience before and during competitive sport.

Ask yourself

Exploring your distractions

1. What things tend to upset your focus *before* a game/match? Give an example of the experience or situation and try to describe how it makes you feel and how it affects your performance. Was this distraction external or internal?

2. What distractions bother you *during* the event itself? Again, try to describe how it makes you feel and how it affects your performance. Was this distraction external or internal?

3. Looking back at these two experiences/situations, how would you like to have reacted to them? Remember – you can't change an external distraction but you *can* change how you react to it.

Now that we've identified what feature as your own distractions, let's consider how you can develop more effective concentration skills and so help to deal with them.

Practical concentration techniques: six of the best

Lots of techniques are available to help athletes to focus properly. The ones that we have found to work best are those that narrow the gap between what you're thinking and what you're doing.

1. Press the switch – turn on your concentration

You must *decide* to focus – it won't happen otherwise. A practical way of doing this is to visualise a mental 'switch on' zone before you compete. For example, imagine turning on your concentration switch as you leave the locker room before a game. This focusing technique was used by Martin Corry, the former England and Lions' rugby forward, who said, 'I used to like switching the dressing room light off, to signify the end of our preparations and the start of something new.'[10]

Appying this technique, can you distinguish between 'on' and 'off' zones in your sporting environment? Also, can you imagine switching on your concentration as you leave the changing room?

2. Develop routines

If you want to play consistently well, you need to *prepare* consistently. Pre-performance routines or preparatory action sequences are very common among athletes in individual sports who perform *self-paced skills* – actions executed largely at their own pace and without interference from others. Routines are valuable because they take you from thinking about a skill to actually doing it, one step at a time. For example, if you're a tennis player, you may like to bounce the ball a certain number of times before you serve. By immersing yourself in each step of your routine, you're training your mind to stay in the present moment. Not surprisingly, many athletes have developed rather idiosyncratic routines. For example, rugby player Owen Farrell, the England and British and Irish Lions out-half, has developed the peculiar habit (which fans call the 'evil eye') of repeatedly looking down at the ball and then up at the target, over and over again before a goal kick. When questioned about this quirky preparation routine, Farrell explained, 'The weird, eye thing that you see? I'm drawing a line from the ball to where I want to kick it. I'll keep drawing a line. Then I'll kick the ball along that line.'[11]

Here's an example of a pre-shot routine in golf:

Try for yourself

Developing a pre-shot routine in golf

Step 1: First, you have to *assess* the situation or 'check it out'. The task here is to gather all relevant information before planning your shot. So, you need to pay attention to the lie of the ball, the length of the grass, the direction and speed of any wind blowing, the distance between your ball and your target and the existence of any special hazards.

Step 2: After that, you must *plan* your shot. In this step, you have to decide on the type of shot you'd like to play, the most suitable club for that shot and the best target for the shot. A useful tip here is to *stand behind the ball* while you grip the club and choose a specific target. The important thing is to be decisive, and once the decision is made, to say to yourself, 'That's it: I've made my mind up'.

Step 3: Next, try to 'see' and 'feel' the shot that you would like to play in your mind's eye. For example, can you see the shape of the shot? Can you see it landing and bouncing close to your target? Once you've pictured it in your head, get into the 'ready' position and align your club and body to the target. Then take your preferred number of practice swings.

> *Step 4*: The final step involves addressing the ball, clearing your mind, glancing at the target again and then – letting your shot flow. This final stage of the routine is often quite difficult because it requires a lot of *trust* to move from thinking about your shot to actually playing it.

3. Use 'trigger words'

Trigger words are short, vivid and positively phrased verbal cues that remind you to focus on a specific target or to perform a specific action. For example, golfer Rory McIlroy used the word 'spot' when putting at the Open Championship which he won in 2014. As he explained:

> I pick a point maybe two or three inches in front of the ball . . . I just try to roll it over that spot and try to not even think about the outcome . . . because I know if I roll it over my spot, then that's all I can actually – that's all I can do.[12]

4. Visualise what you want to do next

As we explained earlier in the book, many top athletes use their imagination to *see* and *feel* themselves executing key skills in their mind's eye before actually performing them (see *Step two* for practical advice on using imagery). For example, racing driver Sebastian Vettel, a four-time Formula One world champion, closes his eyes and sits in the garage before qualifying laps – rehearsing what he's going to do in the race. This helps him to, 'clear your mind . . . to be in the moment.'[13]

Likewise, former swimmer Michael Phelps, the multi-Olympic gold medalist, used imagery to prepare for what might happen in races, 'Visualisation is important so you don't have any surprises.'[14]

For Vettel and Phelps, imagery helped them to prepare for various possible scenarios, thereby ensuring that they would not be distracted by surprising or unexpected events.

5. Relax and centre your body

Physical relaxation techniques can help you to concentrate more effectively. For example, lowering your shoulders, doing gentle neck-rolling exercises, flapping out the tension from your arms and legs and taking slow deep breaths can lower your centre of gravity and reduce the likelihood of error.

Speaking of errors, one of the biggest mistakes that novices in sports such as golf and tennis make is to hold in their breath while they prepare for a shot. If you do this, your muscles will tense up and your swing will be affected. By contrast, exhaling while relaxing your muscles helps you to concentrate. That's what Jonny Wilkinson, the former England and British and Irish Lions rugby outside-half, discovered in his quest for the perfect way to prepare for a goal-kick:

> As I got more into kicking, I became more involved in looking at other aspects, and one area I looked at was focusing from the inside, slowing down the breathing, relaxation, 'centering', which is a way of channelling my power and energy from my core, just behind my navel, down my left leg and into my left foot to get that explosive power.[15]

6. Get used to distractions when practising: simulation training

As we explained in *Step two* (when discussing Earl Woods' unorthodox approach to helping his son, Tiger), simulation training is based on the theory that athletes will concentrate more effectively in competitive pressure situations if they train under conditions that replicate or mimic them. For example, Bob Bowman, the renowned swimming coach, simulated an unusual pressure situation for Michael Phelps before the 2008 Olympic Games in Beijing. Specifically, he deliberately broke Phelps' goggles before his training races so that he would get used to swimming with his eyes closed if necessary. Amazingly, that exact situation arose when Phelps' googles filled with water during the last 175 metres of the 200-metre butterfly finals at the Games. But because he had been accustomed to swimming blindly in training, Phelps over-came this distraction and won the race.[16]

Applying simulation training to team sports, some techniques for counteracting distractions in football are presented in the following box.

Try for yourself

Simulation training in football: practical suggestions

Distraction	Possible simulation technique
Crowd noise	Playing pre-recorded CDs of crowd noise during training sessions in order to familiarise players with expected distractions during away matches
Gamesmanship	Arranging for team-mates to simulate opponents' gamesmanship during training sessions or practice matches
Fatigue	Alternating normal training sessions with short bouts of high intensity exercise to induce tiredness
Heat/humidity	Arranging for players to train and play while wearing layers of extra clothing to simulate hot weather effects
Unfavourable refereeing decisions	Designing 'modified' games containing deliberately biased umpiring decisions
Pressure	Simulating pressure situations in training (e.g. practising with your team losing 1–0 with five minutes to go)

Resilience and mental toughness: two sides of the same coin

You can't embark on a journey through sport without expecting to encounter adversity in the form of setbacks and failures of different types and at different times. Common sources of adversity include serious injury, making a bad mistake, being dropped from a team or experiencing apparently unfair refereeing decisions, but adversity, by itself, is rarely decisive in athletic competition. What really matters is how you react to it. So, in psychology the term *resilience* refers to how quickly you can bounce back from setbacks and get on with the game. As golfer Gary Player, a nine-time Major winner, once remarked, 'The toughest thing for people to learn in golf is to accept bad holes and then to forget about them.'[17]

As you might expect, resilience is a powerful mental skill that distinguishes successful athletes from less successful counterparts. For example, consider the way in which Retief Goosen, who won the US Open twice, overcame an extraordinary setback in his teenage years. At just 17 years old, he almost died when he was struck by lightning while playing golf. The lightning bolt that hit him was so strong that it welded his clubs together and melted the soles of his shoes. Remarkably, although Goosen spent six days in hospital, he was back playing golf within three weeks of the incident.

The lesson is that whenever setbacks occur, winners not only *get on with it* but actually flourish. And that's why many sport psychologists see *resilience* and *mental toughness* as two sides of the same coin.[18] Whereas resilience is largely *reactive* (overcoming adversity), mental toughness is *proactive* because it involves driving on and flourishing – regardless of whether circumstances are favourable or adverse. A nice example of how resilience and mental toughness go hand in hand comes again from the rugby player Jonny Wilkinson. People usually remember him for scoring the crucial drop-goal that earned England an extra-time, 20–17 victory over Australia in the 2003 World Cup final but what they often forget is that Wilkinson had missed *three* drop-goal attempts in that match before scoring. The lesson here is that despite failing repeatedly, Wilkinson persisted, took control of the situation by calling for the pass before his kick – and eventually succeeded in scoring.

So how can you become more resilient?

Strengthening your resilience – three steps to mental toughness

Bouncing back from adversity requires three key skills – taking control of the situation; having an optimistic outlook; and 'reframing' what happens to you in more helpful terms.

1. Take control

Taking control of what *can* be controlled is vital when adversity strikes. For example, if you suffer a bad injury, it's important to seek advice and take charge of your rehabilitation programme rather than waiting around and feeling sorry for yourself. Similarly, if you're a footballer who loses the ball in a tackle with an opponent, do you wave your hands in frustration and appeal to the referee for a foul – or do you try to win the ball back immediately? Interestingly, when Pep Guardiola was manager of Barcelona FC, he required his players to try to regain possession of the ball *within six seconds* of losing it. This six-second rule proved pivotal to Barcelona's all-conquering, possession-based style of football.

But what happens if you don't try to take control of an adverse situation? Research by the famous psychologist Martin Seligman shows that if we are conditioned by past experience to believe that there is *nothing we can do* to escape adversity, we may develop *learned helplessness* – a fatalistic mindset which makes us think that when similar setbacks occur in the future, failure is inevitable. By contrast, if we're optimistic, and believe that we have even the *slightest* degree of control over a negative situation, we can bounce back from it more quickly and effectively. So, as we'll explain later, learned optimism is the *opposite* of learned helplessness. More generally, many athletes and teams have managed to win matches by staging remarkable recoveries from seemingly impossible deficits. To illustrate, Liverpool FC famously defeated AC Milan in a penalty shoot-out in the 2005 Champions' League final even though they had been 3–0 down at half-time. Likewise, Dennis Taylor won the world snooker championship in 1985 (by 18–17) despite trailing Steve Davis by 8 frames to 0 at one stage. Clearly, the more you take control of a negative situation that affects you, the more resilient you will become.

2. Be optimistic

Optimism – or having a *sunny brain*[19] – is the belief that you can cope with whatever the future may bring. By contrast, pessimism – or having a *rainy brain* – is the gloomy expecation that if anything can go wrong for you in the future, it will. Remarkably, these different styles of thinking have distinctive practical implications for achieving success in sport. For example, Seligman and colleagues discovered that pessimistic swimmers were more likely than equally skilful optimistic counterparts to perform *below* their coaches' expectations over the course of a season. Perhaps more tellingly, the pessimists were also less likely to bouce back from adversity than were the optimists.[20]

So, do you have an optimistic or a pessimistic style of thinking?

Self-assessment exercise

Is your glass half full . . . or half empty?

In order to find out if you're an optimist (you see the glass as half full) or a pessimist (you see the glass as half empty), here's a quick test. It's based on the discovery that we can identify your optimism or pessimism profile by trying to understand how you made sense of bad things that have happened to you, such as a defeat.

Q1. Think of a competition that you lost recently. Do you think that you were personally responsible for the defeat (e.g. because you didn't play well or because you made mistakes) or was it due to some other circumstances?

Q2. If you blame yourself for the defeat, do you think that the weaknesses in your performance will persist in the future?

Q3. How much will this defeat affect other areas of your life?

Analysis

If you think that you were largely responsible for the loss (Q1), that the factors in question (e.g. a poor performance from you) are unlikely to change in the future (Q2), and that the loss will affect many different aspects of your life (Q3), then you probably have a *pessimistic* style of thinking. If so, then you tend to explain setbacks by saying '*I've only myself to blame*', '*It's going to happen again and again*' or '*It's going to ruin my whole life*'. In general, pessimists believe that negative experiences from adversity are their fault, won't change in the future and have far-reaching implications for their lives. Optimists, on the other hand, tend to interpret setbacks as being caused by temporary circumstances which are particular to specific situations and which *can* be changed in the future (e.g. though increased practice and by taking lessons from coaches). The most important point of all, however, is that you can *learn* to be more optimistic by seeing setbacks as temporary misfortunes and by challenging toxic thinking habits. These habits include *overgeneralising* (assuming that because a bad thing happened to you once, it will keep happening in the future), taking things personally (remember – everyone experiences adversity but not all athletes get caught up in self-blame as a result of it) and discounting anything positive (the belief that there are no lessons to be learned from a bad experience).

3. Reframe what happens to you . . . and act accordingly

Reframing adverse situations on your journey – or interpreting them more constructively – can help you to bounce back from them. For example, if you're dropped from a team because of poor performances then you could reframe this setback as an opportuntity to improve some aspect of your game. The challenge here is to ask your coach for specific advice about what to work on so that you can challenge for your place again (see *Step six*).

With this idea in mind, here are some practical tips on reframing setbacks in sport:

Try for yourself

Reframing your setbacks: practical tips

1. **Learn from your mistakes – fail better**. You can't get better at anything without failing. But instead of being embarrassed by your failures, try to *learn* from them. For example, if you made a bad mistake, ask yourself what you would do differently next next time. Remember – it's okay to make mistakes . . . as long as you don't make the *same ones* over and over again! Think of what Nobel prize winner Samuel Beckett said: 'Ever tried. Ever failed. No matter. Try again. Fail again. Fail better'.[21]

2. **Use your disappointments to motivate you**. It's natural to feel disappointed after a setback such as a defeat. But disappointments can be helpful it they motivate you to work harder on a specific part of your game. In short, there's always an 'up side' to feeling down.

3. **Ask yourself what advice would you give to another person in your situation**. What advice would you give to someone who had experienced the same setback as you did? It's surprising how objective we can be when we're looking at other people's problems.

4. **Watch out for wishful thinking**. Stop torturing yourself about what might have been. Wishful thinking can't change anything and stops you from moving on. It's a waste of time.

Overcoming obstacles

In this section, we look at a few common problems that those journeying through sport can encounter. We have tried to offer not only a diagnosis of what these obstacles are but, more importantly, tips on how to overcome them.

'If my first touch goes well, I know I'm going to have a good game but if it doesn't . . . forget it!'

Fortune telling is a form of superstitious thinking which involves predicting the future (in this case, whether or not you're going to play well) on the basis of flimsy or inadequate evidence (here, your first touch). It's a bad habit in sport for at least two reasons. First, it upsets your focus because it makes you think too far ahead, hence distracting you from the task at hand. Second, it can lead to learned helplessness (discussed earlier in this chapter), encouraging you to believe that luck or fate is controlling your performance. On good days, if things start well for you, fortune telling can inspire some initial confidence – but all it takes is one mistake and your whole game could unravel. If this problem applies to you, a good solution is to put yourself centre stage and to highlight the degree of control that you have over your own performance. In particular, in the early stages of competition it's important not to emphasise your first touch but your general work rate and activity.

'I often seem to pick up injuries coming up to big games'

Many sportspeople report picking up niggling injuries in the build up to important games. Sometimes this phenomenon merely reflects heightened self-awareness – the fact that athletes want to ensure that their bodies are just right for the big day. It's a bit like checking that every door and window of your house is locked before you go on holidays. In itself, this sensitivity to bodily signals shouldn't be a major cause for concern, especially when the player has performed well under similar circumstances in the past. On other occasions, however, reports of an injury may act as a psychological insurance policy or ready-made excuse that can be used if the player performs below par – a phenomenon known as *self-handicapping*.[22] A related problem may occur if an athlete's fear of failure creates a mindset where s/he doesn't really want to meet the challenge and so uses the injury as an excuse for crying-off. This problem may call for a more significant intervention to change the player's orientation to competition from a belief such as '*I'll die if I lose*' to one like '*I'll do my best to win*'.

'*If I make a mistake or if something goes wrong for me I can't seem to get it out of my head*'

Many of the issues that we've already discussed can occur in a situation where the spontaneous becomes thoughtful, where thought interferes with action and especially where past mistakes continue to cast a shadow over present performance. The solution is to stay focused on the here-and-now. Look ahead and you lose sight of what you are doing, look behind and you will find that mistakes and *what ifs* will cloud your judgement. With practice, there are many mental skills that can be learned to help you *draw the line* – to consign to history previous mistakes and instead to play it as it comes.

Notes

1. Barnes, S. (1999). Awesome aces sink the marketing gurus. *Irish Independent*, 5 July, p. 14.
2. Syed, M. (2017). *The Greatest; The Search for Sporting Perfection*. London: John Murray, pp. 47–48.
3. Masters, R., & Burns, J. (1995). *Mind Swings: The Thinking Way to Better Golf*. London: Aurum Press.

4. Staph, J. (2011). Usain Bolt's key to explosive starts. *Stack*, 1 March. www. stack.com/a/usain-bolts-key-to-explosive-starts accessed on 13 September 2018.

5. How to . . . psyche out a batsman. *Sky Sports Magazine*, December/January 2011, p. 11.

6. Peter, J. (2018). Mikaela Shiffrin imposes social media blackout during Olympics to limit distractions. *USA Today Sports*, 15 February. https://eu. usatoday.com/story/sports/winter-olympics-2018/2018/02/15/mikaela-shiffrin-imposes-social-media-blackout-during-olympics-limit-distractions/ 340009002/ accessed on 13 September 2018.

7. Slattery, W. (2016). Rory McIlroy reveals the moment he almost walked away from golf, *Irish Independent*, 17 May. www.independent.ie/sport/golf/ i-didnt-want-to-play-anymore-rory-mcilroy-reveals-the-moment-he-almost-walked-away-from-golf-34724839.html accessed on 13 September 2018.

8. Hodge, K. (2000). *Sports Thoughts*. Auckland, New Zealand: Reed, p. 72.

9. Hanin, Y. L. (2014). Iceberg profile. In R. C. Eklund & G. Tenenbaum (Eds.), *Encyclopaedia of Sport and Exercise Psychology*, vol. 1 (pp. 361–366). New York: SAGE.

10. Corry, M. (2007). Brocolli, foul focus drinks and hip-hop: How we will prepare for the big kick-off. *The Guardian* (Sport), 13 October, p. 3.

11. The strangest kicking routines in rugby union. *Telegraph Sport*, 2 March 2016. www.telegraph.co.uk/rugby-union/2016/03/03/the-strangest-kicking-routines-in-rugby-union/

12. How golf champs Rory's trigger words will raise your sales. *Salespodder*. https://salespodder.com/how-golf-champ-rorys-trigger-words-will-raise-your-sales/ accessed on 14 September 2018.

13. Brolin, C. (2017). *In the Zone: How Champions Think and Win Big*. London: Blink Publishing, p. 44.

14. Ibid., p. 40.

15. Williams, R. (2003). It's all in the hands. *The Guardian* (G2), 20 November, p. 2.

16. Linden, J. (2008). Coach reveals tricks he used tp prepare Phelps. *Sports News*, 20 August. www.reuters.com/article/us-olympics-swimming-phelps/ coach-reveals-tricks-he-used-to-prepare-phelps-idUSSP27658220080820 accessed on 14 September 2018.

17. MacRury, D. (1997). *Golfers on Golf*. London: Virgin Books.

18. Gucciardi, D. (2017). Mental toughness: Progress and prospects. *Current Opinion in Psychology*, 16, 17–23.

19. Fox, E. (2012). *Rainy Brain, Sunny Brain: The New Science of Optimism and Pessimism*. London: Heinemann.

20. Seligman, M. E. P., Nolen-Hoeksema, S., Thornton, N., & Thornton, K. M. (1990). Explanatory style as a mechanism of disappointing athletic performance. *Psychological Science*, 1, 143–146.

21. Beckett, S. (1983). *Worstward Ho*. New York: Grove Press.

22. Jones, E. E., & Berglas, S. (1978). Control of attributions about the self through self-handicapping strategies: The appeal of alcohol and the role of underachievement. *Personality and Social Psychology Bulletin*, 4(2), 200–206.

4 Looking back

By now, the guiding principles for your sporting journey are hopefully in place but there is one final ingredient that should never be forgotten – the insight that can be gained from reflecting on the past or where you've been. This is the time to equip you with the tools that will assist you in your future quest but we begin by looking not *forwards* but *backwards*.

To help this process one word must be uppermost in your thoughts: honesty. Too many sportspeople can lose their way because they fool themselves, or others, for example by borrowing others' identities, and especially those who have already achieved success. Former England football player Peter Crouch said he decided to buy an Aston Martin sportscar and drive around with two fingers on the steering wheel telling himself, 'You've never looked cooler'. Meanwhile, Crouch said he was aware of a 'little voice deep down keeps telling me an Aston Martin isn't me'.[1]

Learning from others can be very useful but on your journey you must be at ease with who you are and understand what makes you what you are. Don't worry, we are not about to plunge you into the world of psychotherapy – that's a different journey and can lead you in a very different direction. Some confuse sport psychology with *therapy* but we hope that our toolkit helps to clear up any confusion on this matter.

Likewise, self-assessment does not have to extend to all aspects of personality or temperament but only those directly related to sporting performance and wellness. As *Step one* made clear, *who you are* is at the core of the whole enterprise but we are now concerned with fine-tuning those aspects of *what makes you what you are* so as to maximise your sporting potential.

In essence, we are suggesting the concept of *mirror gazing* or honest self-reflection. As the story goes, many years ago, at the start of his test career a very famous New Zealand rugby player is alleged to have let the rest of the team know exactly what he thought of their poor performances after one particular game. Unwittingly he had broken an unspoken rule among the team at that time. Grabbing him by the throat, the captain shoved his face into a mirror and let him know in no uncertain terms that this behaviour was unacceptable. In fact, in that era no All Blacks player was allowed to discuss the game until he had looked into a mirror and asked himself a vital question – what did I do for the team? Only then had he earned the right to talk to his team-mates.

A powerful lesson. While we all assess our performances from time to time, it is rare that this evaluation will be thorough and systematic. Instead, we are inclined to be naturally selective, choosing aspects of play that we or others consider to be the most important. If your confidence is high then you are likely to focus on the positives but if your confidence has dipped, then you are more likely to highlight your mistakes and weaknesses. In this way you may lose a rounded or balanced picture of performance and come to highlight a small fraction of the total scene. This selective evaluation will then influence how you prepare. In turn this spiral can adversely affect performance as a *self-fulfilling prophecy* and so the cycle of delusion may continue.

The alternative is to use systematic tools to assess what has been done and what needs to be done, which provides the impetus for *self-motivation*. *Performance profiling* and *goal setting* are two valuable techniques for helping an athlete become self-driven or self-motivated but before going any further it may be useful to clarify just what is meant by the term motivation. We have all heard this term used frequently – but do we really know what it means?

Staying motivated

Ask anyone what motivation is and they are quite likely to talk about the things that motivate us, including the motives that make us get out of bed in the morning and do something. In psychology similar ideas have long held sway and so, for example, Abraham Maslow famously described a hierarchical set of needs that motivate or drive us to action.[3]

Moving from bottom to top of Maslow's pyramid or hierarchy, the needs begin with basic survival then safety needs, belonging, esteem and finally, self-actualisation itself. According to Maslow we are only able to deal with higher order needs once we have sorted out the rest.

The model sounds entirely plausible until you test it against the real world and then you often find that life is not quite so orderly. Basically, we make choices and prioritise different motives at different times based on what we *choose* to prioritise. So, for example, the artist may buy canvas at the expense of food, or the explorer may risk life and limb to reach a summit for no other motive than, in the famous words of the ill-fated Everest pioneer George Mallory, 'Because it's there'. These may be exceptional examples but in general we are often far more sophisticated in our decision making and how we prioritise motives than earlier content models of motivation, including Abraham Maslow's, would suggest.

Within sport psychology there have been hundreds of studies aimed at identifying the significance of different motives in determining why we take part in sport. Interestingly, with increasing evidence of obesity and related health problems among young people, an urgent priority is how to encourage young people to take part in physical activity of any sort. Intricate models of participation motivation have emerged to suggest that a whole host of variables interact to determine why we take part and continue to participate, with a critical distinction being made between *extrinsic motives* (doing it for rewards that are outside the individual – such as money, status, trophies) as opposed to motives that come from within or *intrinsic motives* (e.g. feeling good, self-realisation or enjoyment of the activity for its own sake).

In general, this research suggests that intrinsic motives are the most powerful and sustainable over the long term. In short, doing something for the sake of the task itself instead of boosting your ego works best. In many ways, these findings underscore the philosophy outlined in *Step one*.

In recent years, the literature has moved from simple descriptions of motives and drives towards a more complex understanding of how these factors act to move us.[4] These theories and models make reference to issues that can influence our commitment but the core is simple and is worth keeping in mind on your travels. These models describe motivation not in terms of content but as a dynamic *process* – in other words the how and the why of what we do. The process of motivation is seen to hinge on the relationship between four factors (see the following table):

Effort	How hard we are prepared to work
Performance	What we do, in training and competition
Outcome	What we get out of what we do
Satisfaction	How we feel about the process

It is assumed that these four elements relate in a systematic way (see the following).

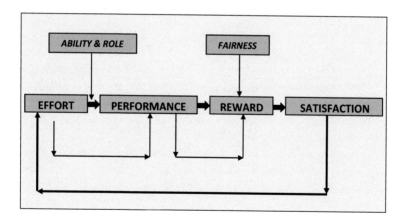

This model is very useful for helping you to understand and diagnose problems that may arise on your sporting journey, including why it is that you or others don't seem to have the same enthusiasm as before, and how this can be remedied.

To explain, in order to be motivated at all, you must recognise that an increase in the *effort* you are prepared to put in can be repaid in a positive change in *performance* – otherwise why bother or make the effort? However, common sense dictates that an increase in effort does not automatically reflect in improved performance. Your *ability* will play a part, as will the *role* that you are asked to play – your position in a team or the style of play you must adopt. You may be highly motivated but if you don't have the knowledge and skills, or you are being asked to do something which is inappropriate, then all your effort will count for nothing.

Next, you must not only believe that an increase in effort can change your performance but also that change, whether during training or in competition, will reflect in *outcomes* or *rewards* that you genuinely value – including both the intrinsic and extrinsic. It is not absolute reward either but what you receive relative to those around you that matters – am I getting as much as, more, or less than the next person? In other words, is it *fair* and so was it worth the effort? For example, if I turn up for training without fail twice a week, work as hard as I can, but never receive an acknowledgement whereas other players swan in when they feel like it, always seem to attract the attention of the coach and are guaranteed their starting place, why should I bother?

Only when you have expended effort, seen the performance and judged the outcomes (including success and failure) do you then evaluate the whole process (was it worth it?) and this evaluation then determines your level of *satisfaction* which in turn determines the effort you are prepared to invest in the future.

As you look across this process, it becomes possible to spot occasions where the chain is weak or broken and so your motivation to continue is reduced or is lost. Is the problem with ability, perceived ability, role, positive feedback on effort and on good performances, fairness? Each of these factors is likely to play some part in sustaining your motivation over time.

How to improve and sustain motivation is the rationale for a highly influential model proposed by psychologists Ed Deci and Richard Ryan.[5] This has helped explain the motivational processes in under-age youth sport[6] as well as sustained success in high performance team sport.[7] Among young participants commencing their athletic careers, 'Positivity should arguably be central, even above technical proficiency or "getting noticed" (e.g. by scouts), if we wish to promote enjoyment and continued participation.'[8]

That said, while other factors like age, grade or context are relevant, Deci and Ryan's three-pronged theory of self-determination (summarised in the following table) provides a sound set of principles for helping foster motivation, underlining once more that motivation is best thought of as a dynamic, ongoing process.

Autonomy	Individuals need to feel a sense of control of their own destiny and that what they are doing is something they have chosen to do
Relatedness	Individuals need to feel a connection with others and be able to satisfy their need for a sense of belonging
Competence	Individuals need to feel that they can become competent in tasks and skills which matter to them and develop a sense of mastery

In this way, successful competitive environments help to bring out the best in players and athletes. By way of example, the manager of the Dublin Gaelic Football team which won its fourth consecutive All-Ireland title in 2018 said that trading off history, past events or jibes from critics and opponents is all gone:

> There's no external, it's all internal motivation. You are not looking for motivation off any other team. You can't control how another team prepare or what they use. It's short lived. It will run itself out. We have always tried to be our best and give our all.[9]

Yet, within the four walls of Dublin's changing room and training area on All-Ireland Final day, the temptation to include external motivation as an added ingredient was still there. On one occasion, a lengthy quote from Charles Darwin's book on natural selection, *The Descent of Man*,[10] was hung on the wall. But this also hints at the fact that individual 'internal' motivation can be closely tied to the identity and culture fostered within a team or club environment – we'll explore more of this in *Step five*.

So, having explained the process of motivation, we must now turn to the *practice of motivating* and how we can encourage and sustain a long-term commitment to continuous improvement on your journey.

Performance profiling

Across top-level sport, the technique of performance profiling (which we mentioned in *Step four*) is now widely accepted as a natural starting point for systematically identifying your strengths and weaknesses – or as we would describe it, your *areas for improvement*. For example, many national sports institutes now routinely provide their élite performers with training diaries or logs in order to make sure that they are able to reference previous performances in moving onwards and upwards – in other words, profiling.

In final preparations for the London Olympics in 2012, Jessica Ennis-Hill was closely profiling her own performance in all events for the heptathlon. From past performances, Jessica knew that she needed to improve in her long jump and javelin to have a chance of fulfilling her dream of Olympic gold. Barely a fortnight before the Olympics began, in her final competitive preparation, she was still carefully monitoring her own performance:

> I'm not pleased with the (long jump) distance but after the trials I had to make changes to make sure I was getting on the board and not fouling. My run up is much better, I just have to work on some flight stuff now. The javelin was good. I'd love to throw a PB (personal best) but I'm happy where I am at this stage. I dont want to have my big throws too early.[11]

What's fascinating here is that Jessica was not fixating on the *outcome* (distance) but instead, was focused on the *process* (i.e. execution of skill). She went on to win Olympic gold.

While profiling has attracted most attention in relation to élite sport, it can be useful in a wide range of other contexts, and at all levels of ability, by refining preparation to optimise performance. At the beginning and end of a campaign or season it is also a useful way of establishing what has been achieved and what is needed in the future. The same techniques employed by athletes can be used by team coaches, where exactly the same principles apply. Indeed, where coaches and athletes work together, profiling provides a helpful framework within which to share and compare reflections on performance, before planning the journey ahead.

Profiling can be implemented in many ways ranging from the highly structured to the less formal. Almost all profiling techniques identify a list of attributes together with scores (e.g. out of 10) to represent where you are and where you would like to be. Richard Butler, an eminent UK sport psychologist, pioneered the use of an interesting device, the performance dartboard, as an easy visual tool for presenting profiles.[12] Each attribute is assigned a segment of the dartboard and within each segment two colours usually represent the scores of '*where you are*' and '*where you would like to be*', typically out of 10. While useful, the number of segments on the board restricts the attributes that can be shown to 20.

As an alternative to the dartboard, a simple chart can be used instead. You can list on the chart all the attributes, skills, knowledge, techniques, etc. that are relevant to performance, and then honestly appraise where you stand in relation to each one.

To help you understand the process, let's use an example of a young golfer who is keen to win a place on the professional tour. She has already decided that she is willing to give this ambition whatever it takes over the next 12 months, and has the full support of her family and coach. The starting point of her journey involves an honest reflection on skills and attributes ranging across the physical to the mental to the tactical, and including lifestyle issues (see the following). You will note that the list doesn't include core aspects of personality or self-identity but instead focuses attention on those skills and issues that are likely to be directly associated with her golf.

Self-assessment exercise

A profiling master plan

	Where am I?	Where do I want to be?
Upper body strength	_____	_____
Leg strength	_____	_____
Bunker play	_____	_____
Putting	_____	_____
Chipping	_____	_____
Driving	_____	_____
Long iron	_____	_____
Short iron	_____	_____
Consistency	_____	_____
Control	_____	_____
Confidence	_____	_____
Commitment	_____	_____
Will to win	_____	_____
Imagery skills	_____	_____
Attentional styles	_____	_____
Lifestyle	_____	_____
Diet	_____	_____
Sleep patterns	_____	_____
Reading a course	_____	_____
Reading a green	_____	_____
Club selection	_____	_____
Shot selection	_____	_____
Relaxation skills	_____	_____

Time management	_____	_____
Fear of failure	_____	_____
Need to achieve	_____	_____
Thought stopping techniques	_____	_____
Physical fitness	_____	_____
Flexibility	_____	_____
Knowledge	_____	_____
Listening skills	_____	_____
Social skills	_____	_____
Media/PR skills	_____	_____

The player could first of all complete the left hand column and then reflect on the right, highlighting occasions where there is the greatest need for improvement. It is important to avoid the temptation of always putting a '10' in the right hand column. Why? Because perfection is often unattainable. Instead it is more sensible to give a realistic assessment of where you'd like to be by a certain date. Having put down where you stand now, it is useful to bring in as many people as possible to give an opinion as to whether the ratings that you have given yourself are accurate and realistic. The completed scale then provides a starting point for a goal setting master plan to move from left to right – from where you are now to where you want to be in the future.

Post-performance profiling

The procedure described earlier will take time and is designed for long-term planning. More immediately, after each competition it may be possible to come up with a shorter list that you could use to judge your performance, and before your next training session. Clearly there is scope in such a procedure to introduce attributes that your coach may highlight and especially if that is an area that the team as a whole really needs to work on. A typical example from a team sport is shown in the following.

Self-assessment exercise

Post-match analysis										
	Your performance (out of 10)									
Work rate	1	2	3	4	5	6	7	8	9	10
Distribution	1	2	3	4	5	6	7	8	9	10
Winning possession	1	2	3	4	5	6	7	8	9	10
Reading the game	1	2	3	4	5	6	7	8	9	10
Defence	1	2	3	4	5	6	7	8	9	10
Support	1	2	3	4	5	6	7	8	9	10
Consistency	1	2	3	4	5	6	7	8	9	10
Discipline	1	2	3	4	5	6	7	8	9	10
Team player	1	2	3	4	5	6	7	8	9	10
Communication	1	2	3	4	5	6	7	8	9	10

By adopting this systematic and personal approach to evaluation you are avoiding the pitfalls attached to focusing exclusively on immediate or high profile issues. It forces a more rounded assessment and can also form a very useful basis for discussion between the player and the coach or manager. Above all, the scores recorded in the profile are the focus for this discussion – not the scoreline in the game or the headline in the post-match report.

If you are a coach it is often useful to have the player complete this post-match analysis alone before sitting down with you and talking through scores and what can be done to bring about an improvement.

Providing constructive feedback on performance profiles is another very valuable way to enhance communication itself, and underpinning this with honesty.

For coaches and athletes alike, performance profiling techniques are not difficult to learn but more than anything, they require the ability to offer an honest appraisal of your strengths and areas for improvement. A training log or diary could be used to support these profiles, providing comments on reasons why your performance may have dipped or peaked at certain times.

'Que sera sera'

For some athletes, these profiling techniques will be immediately welcome as they help to reinforce their existing practices based on principles of personal control and agency – in other words, *doing something about it*. For those who are less analytic, there may be more resistance as the uncertainty attached to each performance continues to offer an unhealthy allure.

Que sera sera (translated as *whatever will be, will be*) is a sentiment that many sportspeople seem to buy into all too readily. It can be comforting to believe that the finger of fate can point in your direction at some happy and unexpected time and so long as you hang in there, things may change for the better. National lotteries thrive on this sentiment – coupled with our poor understanding of statistics. However, in sport this mindset becomes a recipe for inconsistency and not improvement. Many sportspeople cling to rituals and superstitions (see also *Step three*) before they compete in the belief that these will *magically* reduce the risk of failure.

When used properly pre-performance routines can improve control, commitment and confidence (see *Step one*) but if used as superstitious crutches they can actually increase the risk of failure by taking personal responsibility out of the equation and replacing it with reliance on an external force or authority. Putting your faith in luck or fate automatically reduces the scope for accepting personal control and thereby doing something about it. In relation to goal setting and self-motivation this can create serious obstacles to progress.

Dealing with these issues can be difficult and they often have to be handled extremely sensitively. Fortunately, reliance on these rituals will tend to decline as the foundations of an effective intervention are laid down – but they can quickly reappear and especially during times of particular stress, seemingly as a way of controlling anxiety. Again, perversely, reliance on superstition or fate will have precisely the *opposite* effect in the longer term by taking the person out of the driving seat and turning them into a backseat passenger. In this scenario, anxiety and worry based on the uncertainty of outcome will flourish.

Before we continue, please do not imagine that we are in the process of fashioning a sporting android, devoid of human feelings and personality. Nothing could be further from the truth. The purpose is quite the opposite, to put you as a person first – but in control and stripped of the baggage that conspires to hold you back. Asking someone to reflect on their performance is not an alien task. We all look back on what we have done well and badly but often we do this haphazardly and in a way that reinforces false impressions. The lesson is clear – if you profile your performance systematically, it becomes an aid to progress on your travels and not a barrier. In this way, honest reflection through performance profiling can help you direct your energy and attention to self-improvement. Former Irish international rugby captain Paul O'Connell found that by applying these same principles, he improved his playing career:

> I got much better at the process that went into winning, rather than being distracted by thoughts of what winning or losing might feel like. For me the process became the key to high performance and, just as importantly, the key to enjoying the whole journey.[13]

Setting goals

Knowing where you stand in terms of relevant skills, knowledge and attributes, and then identifying where you need to be, is obviously critical but the next step is even more so – finding a way of travelling from here to there.

Interestingly, the most successful Olympic swimmer of all time, Michael Phelps, very publicly set himself the goal of winning seven gold medals in the 2008 Olympic Games – to add to the six he had already won in Athens. He duly won eight! London 2012 was his last Olympics. Was goal setting still important to the man known as *The Baltimore Bullet*? As he said in 2011:

> The goal I have set for London is a very hard goal. I think it's something that I think I can reach, and it will mean something very special if I reach that. The only two that are really going to know that goal are Bob [Bowman, his coach] and I. We're the only two that are going to put the countless hours in the pool and the weight room.[14]

Michael duly won four golds and two silvers at the London Olympics, to become the most decorated Olympian of all time (22 medals, 18 gold), before subsequently announcing his retirement.

Within sport, goal setting really came to life in the 1970s. Probably the most famous example of a systematic goal setting procedure was that undertaken by the 1976 Olympic gold medallist, John Naber.[15] John succeeded not only in winning his gold medal in the 100m backstroke but also three other golds and a silver medal – and broke four world records in the process.

Case study

John Naber: realising his dream

'In 1972 Mark Spitz won seven gold medals, breaking seven world records. I was at home watching him on my living room floor. And I said to myself at that time, "wouldn't it be nice to be able to win a gold medal, to be able to be a world champion in Olympic competition". So right then I had this dream of being an Olympic champion. But right about then it became a goal. That "dream to goal" transition is the biggest thing I learned prior to Olympic competition – how important it is to set a goal. My personal best time in the 100 back was 59.5. Roland Matthes, winning the same event for the second consecutive Olympics (1972), went 56.3. I extrapolated this, you know, three Olympic performances and I figured in 1976, 55.5 would have been the order of the day. That's what I figured I would have to do. So I'm four seconds off the shortest backstroke event on the Olympic program. It's the equivalent of dropping four seconds in the 440 yard dash. It's a substantial chunk. But because it's a goal, now I can decisively figure out how I can attack that. I have four years to do it in. I'm watching TV in 1972. I've got four years to train. So it's only one second a year. That's still a substantial jump. Swimmers train ten or eleven months a year, so it's about a tenth of a second a month, giving time off for missed workouts. And you figure we train six days a week so it's only about 1/300 of a second a day. We train from 6–8 in the morning and 4–6 in the evening so it's really only about 1/1200 of a second every hour. Do you know how short a 1/1200 of a second is? Look at my hand and blink when I snap my fingers, would you please? Okay, from the time when your eyelids started to close to the time they touched, 5/1200 of a second elapsed. For me to stand on the pool deck and say, "during the next 60 minutes I'm going to improve that much", that's a believable dream. I can believe in myself. I can't believe I'm going to drop four seconds by the next Olympics. But I can believe I can get that much faster. Couldn't you? Sure!! So all of a sudden I'm moving.'

Source: Fletcher, D. (2006). British swimming, sports psychology, and Olympic medals: It's all in the mind. *The World Swimming Coaches Association Newsletter*, 6, 5.

Use of goal setting as a motivational technique in sport can be traced directly back to a theory initially developed in the world of business[16] where it had long been regarded as an essential tool in motivational training programmes. Since that time basic goal setting procedures have become increasingly popular and accessible to sport coaches and athletes alike. Not surprisingly the principles have been translated into popular language in order to encourage practical use.

While goal setting can and often does work well, it is not without problems. However let's begin by suggesting how these principles may be applied – before issuing a few health warnings based on our practical experience of working with goal setting in sport over many years.

Goal setting research has been carried out in a wide variety of situations but regardless of the type of task or the individuals tested, the majority of studies reveal that setting goals can lead to improved performance. As to why, goals probably have a positive influence in at least four ways. First, they focus attention; second, they mobilise effort in proportion to task demands; third, they enhance persistence; and finally, they encourage the adoption of longer-term strategies. Furthermore, a number of goal setting principles enhance these performance effects (see the following).

Summary

Goal setting principles	
Difficulty	More difficult goals lead to a higher level of performance than easy goals.
Specificity	Specific goals are more effective than general subjective goals (e.g. 'do your best') or no goals.
Acceptance	To be effective goals must be accepted by the performer whether they are self-instigated or assigned by someone else.
Feedback	Goals will not be effective in the absence of feedback.

While not all of us may have the single-minded dedication of a John Naber or other great Olympians,[17] we can still draw on broadly similar principles to establish goals that will lead like small stepping stones along the route from where we are to where we want to be. Having profiled your performance or your skills/knowledge, you have already made considerable progress in delivering on goal setting. However, just because you can measure your progress does not mean that you are committed to action. So before going any further, it is worth pausing to answer the following questions:

> **What would you like to achieve in your sport?**
> **How important is it to you?**

If your sporting goal is really not all that important to you, then there is no point in putting in place a regime that is doomed to failure before it even begins. This is not an admission of defeat but a realistic and sober assessment of what is important in your life and where your priorities lie. To downgrade sport to a recreational activity, and then to invest an appropriate amount of time and energy in something that still matters, is fine. There may still be scope for limited goal setting even in these circumstances. The current trend of exercise programmes such as *Couch to 5k* could be one example of this.

However, if you have the commitment to continue to improve, the next stage is to return to the results of your performance profiling. One at a time, identify each item on the list/profile where there is room for improvement then prioritise these items in a sensible way which allows you to draw up a goal setting master plan.

When is the best time to do this work? It is not during the heat of competition or following a run of poor form. Instead goal setting plans are best devised during the close or off-season, when you have had an opportunity to reflect on where you are going and how you are going to get there.

Your master plan should include a timescale for each skill, attribute or area of knowledge, indicating where you are and where you want to be by a given date. The timescale, start date and end point for each should be tailored to your unique circumstances, always taking into account practical considerations and including the time and resources you have available. To keep this scheme in your thoughts, this plan could be presented on a large sheet which is pinned somewhere prominently to constantly remind you of your schedule. Different types of goals relate to different stages of your season and career, as Olympic champion Jessica Ennis-Hill explained:

> I sit down with my coach and we kind of plan short term goals, so what I want from my indoor season, what competitions do I want to do and what I want to get out of them. And then long term goals for year upon year . . then during a Heptathlon, you kind of know where you're at from your training and what you roughly want to get from each event.[18]

From a practical perspective, a *Gantt Chart*[19] offers a simple way of representing different timelines for different goal setting activities. Many commercial software packages are now available to make the task of constructing a chart very easy and this will allow you to see immediately the start and end points for each programme, and also significant checkpoints along the way. The chart will also allow you to describe connections between the various activities. For example, you may wish to develop strength and flexibility before working on a particular skill or routine.

Something else may happen when you put down on paper what you want to achieve and the steps which must be taken to achieving it – you become *accountable*. Accountability helps to foster honesty and as we've said, honesty is essential to learning and improvement. It may also be that sharing goals and actions to fulfill them fosters *relatedness*. Increasingly teams use social media platforms such as *Whatsapp* or *Instagram* where players may post pictures of individual training sessions. But social media is also open to abuse and misuse. Simplicity is the key here. Having made a breakthrough as Olympians in 2016, the O'Donovan brothers won gold in the 2018 World Rowing Championships in Plodiv. However, their jocular, fun-loving post-event commentary may belie a competitive edge and professional approach to preparation which lies hidden beneath the surface:

> All the athletes on the Irish (rowing) team, all year around, they've shown great independence. They've taken fierce responsibility on

themselves, you know, and accountability for their own training and accountability for their own results. It's evident that the team has belief and the athletes have belief. It's been coming a long time.[20]

This perspective of accountability neatly fits with the idea of autonomy, touched upon earlier. Coming from the inimitable and enthusiastic O'Donovan brothers, it also shows accountability need not be humourless to aid success!

Doing goal setting

Having established a goal setting masterplan, now is the time to look at each of its elements in more detail. To do this, for the sake of convenience the principles are often presented as an acronym, either *SMART* (specific, measurable, attainable, realistic and timely) or *SCAMP* (more correctly *SCCAMMP!*). Of the two, we have found that the latter (see following table) seems to capture the principles more completely, and sits easily alongside the philosophy we have outlined earlier.

Try for yourself

SCCAMMP!

S = Specific

Don't set vague goals, e.g. get better. Specify exactly how much you want to improve and how you can measure it. Predict the extent of your improvement and you will work hard to achieve it.

C = Challenging and Controllable

Set performance goals at a level slightly ahead of your current ability; this means that goals are possible but also provide an interesting challenge. Also remember to keep your goals within personal control rather than depending on performance of others (e.g. performance not outcome).

A = *Attainable*

Don't burden yourself with an impossible goal. All goals should relate to where you are now and you should aim to improve yourself step by step. Don't be afraid to reassess goals if they prove to be unrealistic.

M = *Measurable and Multiple*

A sense of achievement is greatest and motivation enhanced most effectively when progress can actually be seen. Goals are best expressed in a form which can be measured objectively, e.g. seconds off time. Failing that, measure performance or characteristic on a subjective rating scale of 1 to 10, e.g. rate ability to cope under pressure on a scale of 1 to 10. Also, multiple goals increase the probability of achievement.

P = *Personal*

The goals you set must relate to you as an individual. Decide what you want to achieve; don't borrow other people's goals. This will enhance your commitment to these objectives.

To see what this can mean in practice, we will use the example of a tennis player who decides, among many other things and in consultation with her coach, that she wants to improve her first serve accuracy.

Case study

Goal setting in action

An up-and-coming tennis player wishes to improve the accuracy of her first serve. At present she determines that when serving at maximum speed, on average she is able to hit the ball into an imaginary two-metre target circle in the receiving court three times out of ten. She then sets herself a realistic goal of being able to hit this target seven times out of ten by the start of the season, in ten weeks time. How does she achieve this? She works out a training programme that involves going to an empty court at her local club three times a week and on each occasion hitting 80 serves, 40 shots from each side of the court into four imaginary targets (ten per target) on each visit. She establishes weekly targets and records her performance on each occasion, including subjective rating, and charts her improvement over time. In the light of this continual feedback she is able to check whether she is on line for achieving her goal and can adjust her practice over the weeks if necessary.

Exactly the same principles can be applied to any sport and any skill, whether related to preparation or performance itself. Using goal setting in training or in the off-season may also have different potential benefits. Former Australian Rules footballer Jim Stynes hailed from Ireland. Winter training in his youth would take him into the exposed, moutainous terrain around his native Dublin. Without obvious milestones, Stynes described how he built his stamina by breaking down his up-hill 20km run using physical markers around him:

> I would pick out something like a telephone pole on the road ahead, and my mind would then convince my legs and lungs to go their hardest until the pole had been reached. Then another target on the horizon would be identified. And so it went, one telegraph pole at a time.[21]

Goals can also be directly related to developing skills specific to your role. Long before Steph Curry became a household name in the NBA, he was among a group of young high school 'shooting guards' invited to a skills academy hosted by basketball star Kobe Bryant. At the end of each training session, Curry would not leave the court until he had swished five free throws in a row.[22] Curry set this goal for himself and then monitored his own performance.

The rules of goal setting are simple. By answering each of the following ten questions you should be able to develop a goal setting programme for every skill or quality that you would like to improve.

Ask yourself

The ten-step approach to goal setting

1. Which aspect of performance do I wish to improve?
2. What associated skills/qualities/attributes must be developed?
3. What routines or practices will help me improve each of these?
4. How can I measure each routine/practice?
5. What is my present level of attainment?
6. What level of performance would I like to achieve by a certain date?
7. What milestones do I want to put in place between the start and the end?
8. What level of performance do I want to reach by each milestone?
9. Who can help me monitor my progress?
10. Who can provide me with expert advice to 'quality assure' the process?

For each item on a profiling list, it may be that one or several goal setting procedures are relevant. For example, under the label of *flexibility* there may be several stretching routines that you follow for different muscle groups. More generally, the same principles still apply for each procedure. You establish a baseline (e.g. how far beyond my big toe can I reach on a toe-board?), you then establish your goal by a given date (e.g. a further ten centimetres in two weeks) and then put in place milestones along the way at which time you measure and thereby establish and record progress made (e.g. ticks or stars on the Gantt Chart).

Timetables can and should be modified to take into account changing circumstances including illness, injury or other commitments. Never forget that this procedure is designed to make you feel good about reaching targets – it is not about hurting yourself when you fail. If the programme is too difficult or over-optimistic then always adjust, and never be afraid to seek advice from others.

Some skills or qualities are easy to measure while others are more difficult. Strength or physical ability can usually be measured without too much difficulty, for example by the number of repetitions, weight lifted or accuracy of performance. However, for certain lifestyle issues the means of measurement may be quite different. Sleep patterns may be no more than recording time to bed and time to wake up, having first established what is an appropriate regime. Dietary assessment may involve measurement of calories or type of food (and it should be immediately obvious that many diet clubs actually do no more than simple goal setting when trying to encourage weight loss).

The assessment of other skills or qualities may require more imagination, especially in relation to mental skills. However, with skills such as stress management (e.g. timing pulse rate), reaction time (e.g. timing performance on simple and complex reaction time tasks) or mental rehearsal (e.g. checking the match between the imagined and actual time it takes you to perform a certain task), it can be fun coming up with interesting ways to measure and chart performance. When all else fails it may be a question of resorting to a subjective assessment of how you are feeling, or asking others to rate your performance against specified criteria.

You don't have to do this alone. Talk to other people and especially those with expert knowledge to make sure what you are doing is sensible, and try to involve them in assessment at the milestones to reassure yourself that your improvement is not fiction but fact. At the end of the day it is about you feeling good about your improvement – rather than waiting for others to applaud.

Goal setting and the real world

So far, all may appear rosy. Goal setting looks like a relatively simple psychological technique that will allow you to maximise your potential through structured planning and training. Unfortunately this optimistic presentation can flatter to deceive.

The problem is that goal setting is a prime example of a technique whose popularity is based on *perceived* value but where application has proceeded without acknowledgement of significant theoretical and practical problems. This is not to abandon the approach but instead to suggest that it will only work and be effective in certain circumstances and for certain people.

Some problems stem from the way in which sport differs from the world of work where goal setting was originally developed. For example, there may be obvious differences in the reasons why people are actually involved in either work or sport in the first place. Most importantly, the *extrinsic rewards* associated with work stand in contrast to the *intrinsic motivators* that are so crucial in maintaining a voluntary involvement in many sports.

A further problem arises from the way in which goal setting is applied in sport and in work, especially with regard to the relative emphasis on either *product* or *process*. Performance enhancement in business is normally directly related to an end product – increased productivity or profit. By contrast, goal setting in sport tends to focus on process or performance and not on outcome.

There is also debate in the literature as to whether setting distant, long-term goals can actually be de-motivating in the short term and so whether there is a need to introduce sub-goals in order to sustain commitment. Our earlier discussion strongly suggests that while the long-term goals may light the fire, it has to be constantly rekindled by short-term goals that are within easy reach.

In recent years, coaches in different sports have increasingly advocated the performance benefits of short-term goals and small improvements. For example, former England rugby coach Clive Woodward described these as the *critical non-essentials*[23] and the performance director of the successful British Olympic cycling team Dave Brailsford famously called them *marginal gains.*[24] In psychology these are sometimes called *micro goals.* Not only may such goals be easier to achieve, they may also seem more attainable and satisfying than other goals. In turn, this can help reinforce your motivation to achieve more. That's why *to-do* lists can work well. While swimmer John Naber used his 'eye-blink' strategy to reach his personal goal, this approach may translate to team sport also. This is how Irish International rugby player Rob Kearney thinks: 'If I can improve myself even by 1% then I will improve my own performance . . . and then you are adding more to the team.'[25] Kearney has won four Six Nations championships with his country and is one of only two players on the Irish rugby team to win both Grand Slam titles in 2009 and 2018. His relentless focus on *the one percenters* appears to work well. So it seems one of the best ways to achieve big is to think small!

The last word

On their own sporting journeys, only a dedicated minority could ever hope to match the single-minded dedication shown by some élite sportspeople, including former Olympians such as John Naber. So putting in place such a highly structured programme is probably not feasible for many of us. This is where a strong dose of realism is required. Whichever profiling and goal setting schedules are put in place, they must be tailored to the needs and characteristics of the individual and his or her journey. The flexibility of profiling and goal setting to accommodate individual differences is often ignored and too many schemes have failed as a consequence. Put simply, you have to constantly adjust and readjust these motivational tools in order to meet changing times and changed people as your voyages through sport continue.

Surprisingly, some critics of goal setting claim that it can interfere with competition unless handled with care. For example, a swimmer may be delighted when finishing last in a heat or final simply because s/he had met their individual time target – perhaps a '*PB*' (personal best). Here it's as though rival swimmers had disappeared from the race and the competiton had been reduced to nothing more than an individual time trial!

To counter this unhelpful trend some swimming coaches advocate a shift away from over-reliance on specific performance goals and towards an accommodation of competitive goals, that is, to beat the person in the next lane. Remember that many of the techniques we describe in this chapter are a *means to an end*, and the end is tied to the intrinsic significance of competition itself. This is what makes sport enjoyable, and when the balance becomes tilted so dramatically that winning loses any emotional significance then there are problems.

Nevertheless, even arbitrary goals may make a difference. For example, marathon runners often set goals based on running under a certain time. In fact, competitors are filtered through the start line based on their projected race time. Marathoners often choose round number times as their goals (either a half-hour goal or hour goal).[26] So common is this that some runners define themselves according to their time; for example '*I'm a "sub-four hour" marathon runner.*'

Interestingly, research analysing the distibution of finishing times shows that marathon runners are 1.4 times more likely to finish at one minute *before* four hours (3hr 59m) than at one minute *after* four hours (4hr 01m). Simply put, if you have set a goal of finishing under four hours in a marathon, you're likely to exert extra effort to finish just under that time than just after it.[27]

Then there are scenarios for which goals must change. One of these is injury. Take the example of British triathlete Tim Don. Having set a new Ironman world record in May 2017, Don planned to compete in the Ironman World Championships in Kona, Hawaii. Two days before his race Don was knocked down by a car while he was cycling and broke his neck. His goal of competing for podium position in Kona was crushed in the process. Don's story, retold in his film *The Man with the Halo*, is a remarkable example of courage and resilience. Focusing on his recovery, he reset his goals and six months later finished the Boston marathon in well under three hours.[28]

As this example illustrates, goals can enhance motivation for an injured athlete but great care is required to ensure that the goal set by the athlete complements the injury recovery programme leading to a full return to competition. Sometimes arbitrary goals in these circumstances, such as being fit for a race or competition, can have adverse effects. Novak Djokovic admitted that he had returned from an elbow injury too early and this had undermined his self-confidence.[29] Fortunately, Djokovic made the necessary changes to return to good form in time to become Wimbledon champion in 2018, and reflected afterwards in a very public way on his comeback:

> For the last 2 years, I wasn't patient with my tennis expectations. I wasn't wise in strategising. And I certainly wasn't hearing my body telling me there was something serious happening with my elbow. I was trying to find solutions somewhere else and solution was always inside of me.[30]

Does all this mean that goal setting should be abandoned? No, but it does remind us that it is not a magic wand. Many highly motivated athletes may not need the rigours of a goal setting programme to maintain their commitment. In fact, such a programme may do no more than heighten their anxieties or raise unrealistic expectations. Likewise, rigidity in goals pursued – without regard to other changes, such as injury – may be counter-productive.

At the other end of the ability spectrum, there may be recreational athletes who would find a regimented goal setting programme to be more of a turn-off than a turn-on. Ultimately, we suggest that goal setting can be a powerful tool for sustaining self-motivation but it should be applied with a modicum of common sense and should be tailored to the needs and circumstances of the individual. As we have seen, there are many variations in goal setting practices. The secret of success is to find and use the ones which work best for you.

On our travels we may spend time reflecting on what has been and what could be, and what separates those who dream from those who truly achieve – but there's a difference between *daydreaming* and *reflecting with purpose*. Recognising the difference is the first step to closing the gap between what has been and what could be. And this idea brings us back to a key theme of *Pure Sport* – honesty.

The end?

Pure Sport presents a practical guide to your travels through the world of sport. However, this journey is fundamentally different from many others that you may have taken for one simple reason – *it should never end.*

Why? Two reasons spring to mind. First, until now you've largely been a passenger as we have tried to steer you through the landscape of sport psychology. From now on, things should start to change as you sit in the driver's seat and take hold of the wheel as your personal journey really begins.

The second reason why this chapter does not signal an end is that skill development is not passive and linear but is an active *cyclical* process of constant reflection and renewal. In other words, you have to *keep making it happen* – not waiting for it to happen to you.

Probably the greatest national hunt jockey of all time, Tony McCoy, amazed the racing world by his insatiable hunger for more winners. Graciously receiving accolades, but not allowing them to stand in his way, Tony provides the simple key as to how he was able to keep renewing and re-energising himself before he finally retired:

> I found it hard to accept that all the tributes were about me, but back came that old chestnut about me burning myself out and the possibility of snapping mentally and physically. I know it was well meant, but I also know that I've got the best job in the world and the easiest lifestyle – because it's the one I choose.[31]

In other words, he enjoyed what he was doing and he was choosing to continue doing what he did best, ride horses. It's that simple.

Take another example from the world of motor racing. Sebastian Vettel, who, at 25 years of age, became the youngest ever three-times Formula One World Champion in November 2012. He is very clear about what keeps him coming back for more. It is not the prestige, the glamour or the money, it is his undiluted passion for racing:

> You need passion to succeed. Yes, being a racing driver is a special job but, generally, if you don't like what you do then you're not

going to be very good. You will face a point inside you where you think, "Is this the right thing? Why am I doing this?" . . . Money can be a motivation but it will never make you happy.[32]

A related lesson from sport is worth repeating at this point. If you want it all to be over, or if you mindlessly play down the clock, then you run the risk of undoing all your previous good work. As an old saying goes, don't count time – make time count! Also, remember an earlier message – when the going gets tough, the tough keep doing what got them there in the first place.

Where does all this leave you now? Well, as a reminder, let's return to where we began with *Pure Sport*. Remember that the voyage of exploration that we have tried to chart has one goal in mind – to help you realise your sporting potential. If you feel that you have come to the end of that journey and you have nothing left to discover, then we've failed! Alternatively, as long as you stay actively involved with sport, in whatever role, this journey should never end but should keep driving you onwards and upwards.

Across all sports, there have been many examples of those who failed to test their true potential because they mistakenly felt that they had already reached the end of the road, maybe having achieved a significant goal. Instead they should have paused, celebrated and then duly acknowledged that it was no more than one more stop along the way. On any journey there will be times when you may choose to rest and admire the view but eventually the desire to travel on should stir you to stand up and move on. Without that desire or hunger to journey and see what lies ahead, you are settling for a comfortable life rather than a challenging one – and you should contemplate putting your feet up. In the words of football manager supreme, Alex Ferguson, 'The past is never enough. A victory only lasts a moment. It's where the next one is that matters.'[33]

Flick back through the pages of *Pure Sport* and you'll see that *nowhere* do we signal an end point but a whole series of new beginnings including all the techniques and skills that you continue to develop and carry with you on your sporting travels. To paraphrase the great writer and traveller, Robert Louis Stevenson, it is the journey not the destination that really matters, 'Little do ye know your own blessedness; to travel hopefully is a better thing than to arrive and the true success is to labour.'[34]

Speaking of a journey, along the way you know that you will meet with good times and with bad times, and both should matter to you – but neither too much. After all, without the one (failure), you can never really enjoy the other (success) (see *Step one*). Interestingly, with the right attitude, you will continue to learn far more from your disasters than from your triumphs. In the words of Rudyard Kipling's poem '*If*', you should strive to learn to, 'Treat those two imposters just the same'.[35]

Remember also that to make your sporting journey as enjoyable as possible, you must travel light (see *Step three*). Experienced travellers know that they move most easily and quickly with the least amount of baggage. Let's face it, if you are carrying someone else's luggage and heading for a destination that was not your choice in the first place, the journey is likely to be both tedious and pointless. As a quick reminder, bring to mind these two questions from *Step one* – why are you doing it? (chiefly for love or enjoyment) and who are you doing it for? (chiefly yourself). These questions provide the simple foundations on which to build and sustain a successful sporting career.

Your kit bag

As we have already made clear, travelling light on your sporting journey is critical but there are two small pieces of equipment that you may need to have with you on this adventure. The first is a mirror. This is not to admire yourself or to check who may be coming up behind. Instead, you must use it as a constant way of reminding yourself just *who you are* and *where you are*. Lose sight of a realistic and honest sense of self-identity and trouble lies around the corner.

The second piece of equipment you'll need should be hidden well from view. Although it weighs very little, it will keep you moving ahead. It is *your chip*, or to be more precise, your chip on the shoulder (see *Step one*). Don't regard this as a character flaw or mistakenly confuse it with arrogance or over-confidence. The chip is a positive indication that whatever has been achieved is never quite enough, and this inner drive continues to fuel the hunger for more.

Those who succeed in sport are never quite content. Here's what Mark Cavendish, one of the most fiercely competitive and successful sprint cyclists of all time, said during an interview at the end of his incredible 2011 season, 'I still want more'. To him, the challenge itself remains his inspiration and driving force:

> I never think it's going to be difficult, with me there is no thought of emotion, no thought that it might not be possible . . . The only consequence of anything is going to be crossing the finish line first.[36]

What is more, that drive or hunger should never be used as an excuse for sulking when the best laid plans fall apart. Reality can deliver cruel blows but knowing the chip is still fixed on your shoulder is a sure sign that your journey has not come to an end but that you are willing to pick yourself up and move on, learning as you go.

The crude maxim that we offered earlier in *Step one* ('*Feck it, Do it, Think about it*') captures the mindset of someone who is able to go out and perform unburdened by doubt, who keeps analysis in its place but is always willing to learn before moving on, older and wiser. In this way the journey itself becomes inspiring, with you firmly in charge.

The skills involved in goal setting and performance profiling are critical in helping you to stay on track and in giving you systematic ways of continuing to review and move forward. These skills dovetail with many of the other techniques that we have outlined throughout the book. When tailored to your own needs, they should provide you with a personal collection of tools that can help you to continue to explore your sporting potential.

In our experience, many sportspeople and coaches can be too selective or reactive, cherry picking elements that seem most relevant to them at that particular moment. In its worst form, this approach involves throwing in a sport psychologist to address a team at a time of crisis – usually just before an important competition. Not surprisingly these tactics are rarely effective for at least three reasons. For a start they convey a message to players that psychological preparation is not really their responsibility but is best left to an 'expert' outsider. This problem is especially likely to occur at élite-level sport where players often have so much specialist assistance available to them that they can unwittingly become helpless and indecisive. Second, calling in a sport psychologist at the last minute suggests that proper mental preparation is a quick fix rather than a systematic philosophy. Finally, in our experience any short-term benefits that may be gained from hearing a fresh voice prior to a big match are likely to disappear quickly unless players are persuaded to buy into the entire package.

And that package is precisely what we have tried to explore in this book. Put simply, we hope that *Pure Sport* has shown you how to identify and assemble the mental elements of sporting excellence. Piece by piece, we have hoped to reveal the jigsaw that is commonly known as sport psychology but which actually encompasses the bringing together of thoughts, feelings and actions in the creation of high-quality and consistent sporting performance.

Overcoming obstacles

In this section, we look at a few common problems that those journeying through sport can encounter. We have tried to offer not only a diagnosis of what these obstacles are but, more importantly, tips on how to overcome them.

'I can't raise my game for anything other than the big occasion'

Sometimes, those who have 'been there and done that' may start to become complacent and lose the capacity to raise their game for anything other than the biggest stage. If this problem has ever applied to you, then one way of sharpening your 'edge' is to learn to shift your focus away from outcome or results and towards personal performance targets. For example, if you're a footballer who's played hundreds of matches, it's difficult to sustain the work rate that you showed in your first game – unless you give yourself a 'personal best' challenge. Put simply, this means trying your best to work harder and be more active in aspects of your game today than you did yesterday. For example, can you win more tackles in your next game than you did in your last one?

Explicit performance objectives expressed in activity levels are very useful in these circumstances because they remind us of our personal contract. Alternatively, you may need to shift focus from internal to external, and so become more involved in the management and general well-being of other team-mates. This should have a positive effect on motivation and commitment, especially in situations where players have developed the habit of being critical of less experienced team-mates.

'I can't get to sleep before a game'

This is a common problem that is often made worse before competition because we try so hard to have a good night's sleep – for example, we go to bed earlier than usual and in the process disrupt our normal sleep patterns. The result – we end up tossing and turning and simply can't shut down.

The first rule for getting to sleep is don't break with routine. Before competition, always go to bed at the usual time and not too early. Second, try this simple way for drifting off, known as 'chaining'. You have to concentrate hard on this technique but with practice it can be very effective in a matter of minutes. The trick is to simply allow your mind to drift effortlessly from one thought or image to the next without ever questioning why or reflecting where the chain is going. It can be random, it can be circular but never question just allow your mind to drift, until you will find you drift into sleep. Another useful technique to break vicious cycles of thought is to think back over your day, never stopping to evaluate events but simply ordering what happened and when, in minute detail. Again, once the chain of thought that held your attention is broken, sleep can quickly follow. If all else fails, don't lie there and worry, get up, have a hot drink, and go back to bed when you feel ready.

'Show me the money!'

The tangible rewards attaching to modern sport can often interfere with performance in many unusual ways. At some stage of a career it is often important to stand back, reassess and remind yourself the reason why you play sport in the first place. If enjoyment has moved into second place behind the trappings that go with success then trouble lies ahead, a lesson that the greatest darts player of all time, Phil Taylor, never forgot. The ill-fated England Rugby World Cup squad of 2011 probably don't need to be reminded yet again of this lesson. In the words of three anonymous members of the squad:

> To hear one senior player in the changing room say straight after the quarter-final defeat, 'There's £35,000 just gone down the toilet' made me feel sick. Money shouldn't even come into a player's mind;
> You sense for some players it was more about getting caps and cash than getting better;
> Too many players were chasing endorsements.[37]

With this in mind, it is interesting that one of the coaching team brought in after the debacle of the 2011 World Cup felt his first priority was to put a smile back on the players' faces. According to Andy Farrell:

> I am part of a coaching team that has a responsibility to bring enthusiasm and enjoyment back. The slate has been cleaned, there is no looking back and part of our role is to make sure that the culture in the first week we are together is one of drive and excitement that gets smiles back on faces.[38]

Notes

1. Former England Striker Peter Crouch on the pampered lives of Premier League Players. (2018). *The Times*, 8 September. www.thetimes.co.uk/article/former-england-striker-peter-crouch-on-the-pampered-lives-of-premier-league-players-7l8bjz6kw
2. Merton, Robert K. (1948), The self fulfilling prophecy, *Antioch Review*, 8 (2 (Summer)): 195, doi:10.2307/4609267, ISSN 0003-5769, JSTOR 4609267
3. Maslow, A. H. (1953). *Motivation and Personality.* New York: Harper & Row.
4. Porter, L. W., & Lawler, E. E. (1968). *Managerial Attitudes and Performance.* Homewood, IL: Dorsey Press.
5. Deci, E. L., & Ryan, R. M. (2000). The "what" and "why" of goal pursuits: Human needs and the self-determination of behaviour. *Psychological Enquiry*, 11, 227–268.
6. Keegan, R. J., Harwood, C. G., Spray C. M., & Lavallee, D. E. (2009). A qualitative investigation exploring the motivational climate in early career sports participants: Coach, parent and peer influences on sport motivation, *Psychology of Sport and Exercise*, 10, 361–372.
7. Hodge, K., Henry, G., & Smith, W. (2014). A case study of excellence in elite sport: Motivational climate in a world champion team. *The Sport Psychologist*, 28, 60–74.
8. Keegan et al. (2009). op cit. p. 371.
9. No looking back for Jim Gavin as hand of history rests lightly on his shoulder. *The Irish Independent*, 27 August 2018. www.independent.ie/sport/gaelic-games/no-looking-back-for-jim-gavin-as-hand-of-history-rests-lightly-on-his-shoulders-37254861.html.
10. The motivational words hanging in the warm-up room that inspired Dublin to glory. SportsJOE.ie, September 2016. www.sportsjoe.ie/gaa/the-motivational-words-hanging-in-the-warm-up-room-that-inspired-dublin-to-glory-97658
11. Jessica Ennis delighted after final Olympic preparation at Loughborough. Loughborough University, 9 July 2012. www.lboro.ac.uk/service/publicity/news-releases/2012/130_LEAP.html
12. Butler, R. J. (1996). *Sport Psychology in Action.* Oxford: Butterworth-Heinemann.
13. O'Connell, P. (2016). *The Battle.* Ireland: Penguin, p. 170.
14. Gilmour, R. (2010). London 2012 Olympics: Michael Phelps sets 'hard goal' for Games. *The Telegraph*, 30 July. http://tinyurl.com/ch2n2dz
15. Cited in Fletcher, D. (2006). British swimming, sports psychology, and Olympic medals: It's all in the mind. *The World Swimming Coaches Association Newsletter*, 6, 5.
16. Locke, E. A. (1968). Toward a theory of task motivation and incentives. *Organizational Behaviour and Human Performance*, 3, 157–189.
17. Naber, J. (Ed.). (2005). *Awaken the Olympian Within: Stories from America's Greatest Olympic Motivators.* Irvine, CA: Griffin Publishing Group.

18. Olympic dream: getting into the zone. (30 July 2012). Open University, http://www.open.edu/openlearn/body-mind/health/sport-and-fitness/sport/getting-the-zone
19. Gantt chart. Wikipedia. http://en.wikipedia.org/wiki/Gantt_chart
20. The O'Donovan brothers claim that a night out on the town in Plodiv was what set them up for 'best strokes we ever pulled in our lives'! @RTEsport. *RTE*, 16 September 2018. https://twitter.com/RTEsport/status/104089 7714425233410/video/1
21. Stynes, J. (2012). *My Journey*. Ireland: Penguin, p. 172.
22. Stephen Curry – success is not an accident. YouTube, 2015. https://m.youtube.com/watch?v=RbsmMnAKeOI
23. Woodward, C. (with F. Potanin). (2004). *'Winning!'*. Great Britain: Hodder & Stoughton.
24. How 1% performance improvements led to Olympic gold. *Harvard Business Review*, 30 October 2015. https://hbr.org/2015/10/how-1-performance-improvements-led-to-olympic-gold
25. Rob Kearney: Leadership, meditation and family. *The Irish Times*, 20 April 2015. www.irishtimes.com/business/work/rob-kearney-leadership-meditation-and-family-1.2179513
26. Markle, A., Wu, G., White, R., & Sackett, A. (2018). Goals as reference points in marathon running. *Journal of Risk and Uncertainty*. Chicago Booth University. http://faculty.chicagobooth.edu/george.wu/research/papers/markle%20wu%20white%20sackett%202017%20(goals%20as%20reference%20points%20in%20marathon%20running).pdf
27. Allen, E. J., Dechow, P. M., Pope, D. G., & Wu, G. (2017). Reference-dependent preferences: Evidence from marathon runners. *Management Science*, 63(6), 1657–1672.
28. Tim Don – the man with the halo. YouTube, May 2018. https://m.youtube.com/watch?v=UhjIchwAkAU
29. Novak Djokovic confidence affected by injury. *BBC* (Sport), May 2018. www.bbc.co.uk/sport/tennis/43979116
30. Novak Djokovic opens up on injury, vulnerability, and his 2018 Wimbledon crown. Tennis365, 20 July 2018. www.tennis365.com/atp-tour/novak-djokovic-injury-vulnerability-wimbledon/
31. McCoy, A. P. (2002). *McCoy: The Autobiography* (pp. 265–266). London: Michael Joseph.
32. McRae, D. (2012). Interview: Sebastian Vettel: 'You need passion. Money will never make you happy'. *The Guardian*, 5 March. http://tinyurl.com/6uyte7b
33. McCoy, A. P. (2002). *McCoy: The Autobiography* (p. 266). London: Michael Joseph.
34. Robert Louis Stevenson (1881). Quotation from *Virginibus Puerisque*.
35. Kipling, R. (1895). *If*. (First published in the *Brother Square Toes* chapter of *Rewards and Fairies*, 1910).
36. Fotheringham, W. (2011). Mark Cavendish saddles up for a year when second will be failure. *The Guardian*, 20 November. www.guardian.co.uk/sport/2011/nov/20/mark-cavendish-london-olympics-2012

37. Foy, C. (2011). A team torn to pieces: Sportsmail examines the explosive findings from leaked reports. *The Daily Mail*, 24 November. http://tinyurl.com/cvnb4zk
38. Rees, P. (2011). Andy Farrell plans to make England's players smile again. *The Observer*, 10 December. http://is.gd/6KqOBe

5 | Your teams

Until now our journey has focused almost exclusively on the *individual* as he or she journeys through the world of sport. This work is core to sport psychology and yet individual activity represents only a small part of the story because sport is, at heart, a *social* activity.

With this in mind, *Step five* will lead you in a slightly different direction on your journey and explore the dynamics of sport teams. While previous steps were directed towards self-improvement, the material here focuses on the *collective*, to help you understand the workings of teams and thereby to improve their performance, as well as looking at how we perform in team settings.

Putting the team first

Picking up on this last point, to some people the team is what sport is all about. It is a source of pride and inspiration which makes all the blood, sweat and tears worthwhile. To others, the team element of sport is less important. Indeed there have been many great and talented athletes who never really quite understood the team element of their sport, perhaps for one reason more than any other – individual desire stood in the way of collective ambition.

Everything we have discussed in previous chapters in terms of personal development can flourish in a team environment but only if you are willing to buy wholeheartedly into a critical team value – *collective ambition*. Here, consider the words of John Wooden, one of the greatest coaches of all time, when describing the basketball player Lewis

Alcindor (later Kareem Abdul-Jabbar), the NBA's highest-ever points scorer with 38,387 across his professional career:

> Lewis believed the team came first . . . A great player who is not a team player is not a great player. Lewis Alcindor was a great team player. Why? Because his first priority was the success of the team, even at the expense of his own statistics.[1]

This idea of collective ambition is echoed by the enigmatic football manager José Mourinho:

> Everything is aimed at one thing – the quest for performance. The aim of my form of relationship is not that the players like me, the only objective is the performance of the group. I sacrifice the individual for the collective.[2]

Collective ambition may seem rather abstract but it is not a difficult concept to grasp, it is simply about putting the team and *teamwork* first.

Teamwork

By their very nature, a great many sports rely on *teamwork* and the complex interactions between individual members. Even solitary athletic endeavours (e.g. marathon running, skiing or sailing) commonly involve teams in some shape or form. Take golf, at first glance the archetype of an individual sporting pursuit – just you and the golf course. However, first impressions can be deceptive. On closer inspection we find that top golfers are rarely alone – they travel and work with a large support team of advisors including caddies, managers, agents, physiotherapists, swing coaches, putting specialists – and psychologists. And on occasions, such as the Ryder Cup, they actually play as a team.

In this way popular portrayals of the solitary athlete can be misleading because behind the scenes there will normally be a team involved in setting the person off down the road – and then keeping them on track. Speaking after breaking the single-handed round-the-world record, sailor Ellen MacArthur publicly acknowledged that her solo long-distance voyages across the world's oceans were based on team-work, involving a constant exchange of information with her shore team before, during and after each challenge:

> A record is nothing if not shared. I'm proud of the record but I'm even more proud to be working with the best team in the world. When I was out there I was never ever alone, there was always a team of people behind me, in mind if not in body.[3]

More recently, in 2018 the Formula One racing driver Lewis Hamilton emphasised just how important teamwork had been in helping him become world champion for a remarkable fifth time:

> It really is the teamwork, collectively, you know the unit is just the best I've ever seen in Formula One and I'm pretty sure that sport's ever seen. I'm proud to be a part of that and I'm proud to be a part of that chain that helps win.[4]

In most sports teamwork is seen as something to be encouraged and it is difficult to bring to mind many sports where this is not the case. So what makes good teams and how can individual potential be maximised within a team context?

What is a team?

It would be too easy to gloss over this question because, after all, we each experience teams throughout our lives – but what actually defines a 'team' and, more critically, how justifiable is our inherent confidence in teams (e.g. *'There's safety in numbers'*; *'Two heads are better than one'*; *'Many hands make light work'*)?

To be frank, our experience with teams in many sports suggests it is rare for them to bring out the best in *everyone* if they are simply left to their own devices. Research suggests that small groups rarely per-form at the level of their average member let alone their best member. Despite this, our faith in teams remains unshaken. With this caution in mind, let's first explore what teams are, before considering what they could become. While we may all *know* what a team is, this casual experience is no substitute for careful analysis of the qualities that make teams good, bad or just plain ugly.

In the research literature, you will find teams commonly defined by five features – *interaction, structure, cohesion, goals* and *identity*.[5] Almost any sport team, from the most organised professional club to the most casual get together, will normally qualify on all five counts – but sometimes only just. These features offer a useful starting point for looking at strengths and areas to improve in a team. To show what we mean, think of a team you've been involved with, and then reflect on the following.

Ask yourself

Understanding your team: building a profile

Interaction

During play: Do the players communicate effectively? Is communication generally positive or negative? Who talks and who listens? Is body language positive or negative?

In the changing room: Do team members talk openly? Are they generally quiet or vocal? Who takes the lead? Who makes useful contributions? Is there much banter and how is it taken?

During training: How do team members interact during training? Who speaks and who doesn't, and with whom? Do players volunteer information freely?

Socially: Do the team mix socially – where, when and how frequently? Who socialises and who doesn't? Are there cliques? Do younger and older players mix freely? Who takes the lead and who follows?

Overall, how would you score the team on interaction? ____ (out of 10)

Structure

How long has the team been together? Are there well-defined team roles, both formal and informal? Has the team 'matured' as a working unit? Are those with assigned roles (e.g. captain, vice-captain) good communicators? Who is respected? Who is listened to? Who cracks jokes? Who is usually the centre of affairs? Is there a pecking order within the team? Is the team punctual? Is attendance at training good or patchy?

Overall, how would you score the team on structure? ____ (out of 10)

Task cohesion

As a team, would an observer say they play 'together'? Does the team seem to bring out the best in individual players? Do they give the impression during play itself that they know what to do and how to do it as a unit? Would you describe them as a 'tight' team on the pitch? Is training competitive – is there a healthy edge or are they relaxed?

Overall, how would you score the team on task cohesion? ____ (out of 10)

Social cohesion

Off the pitch, are they a tight group? Are they respectful of each other? Are they exclusive? Do they seem comfortable in each other's company? Are they too comfortable? Do they choose to socialise together?

Overall, how would you score the team on social cohesion? ____ (out of 10)

Goals

Has the team well-defined short, medium and long-term goals? Are they implicit or explicit? Does everyone always seem to pull in the same direction? Are there different agendas at work in the team? Are there dissenting voices or whispers either within the team or among the backroom staff? Does the team stay 'on message' during a game? Is the collective goal stronger than individual goals or priorities? How committed are they to the cause?

Overall, how would you score the team on goals? ____ (out of 10)

Identity

Does the team have an identity (e.g. has it defined its strengths and weaknesses)? Is the team defined by its own qualities or those of others? Is the history of the club or previous teams a help or a hindrance in terms of the team's own identity? Do the key players (e.g. captain) reinforce the identity of the team through what they do and what they say?

Overall, how would you score the team on identity? ____ (out of 10)

By carefully reflecting on your answers, you can start building a team profile and begin to really understand what makes your team tick, while probably becoming aware that terms such as cohesion or team spirit are more complex than you may have first thought.

To explain, there are actually two types of cohesion – task and social. *Task cohesion* is concerned with how well the team works together as a playing unit while *social cohesion* is about how well they get on together socially. These are independent factors and should never be confused – one definitely predicts success, the other is often predicted by success. No prizes for guessing which is which.

It is worth remembering that no two teams will ever be the same – or should ever *try* to be the same. Indeed, even within and around a team, there are changes over time. Awareness of this is important for the ongoing development and improvement of any team over successive seasons. After all, players and athletes are not just performers or competitors, they're people. So too are managers and coaches. In practical terms, this means the management of every team must be tailored to the people involved. Clearly, it is always worth spending time exploring the precise qualities of the group of players with whom you are working before moving forwards too hastily.

The looking glass

Taking into consideration the five team dimensions mentioned earlier, you can begin to reflect on the qualities of the team itself. At this stage, avoid the temptation of labelling the team crudely as being either good or bad. Instead, try to be more clinical in defining your team's strengths and areas for improvement. Only through a systematic evaluation of each one of the five elements will you produce a solid foundation for later work. This can complement the development of performance profiles by individual team members, as outlined in *Step four*. Former All Blacks coach Wayne Smith said that a *strengths-based* approach guided his coaching and became kernel to the team, 'We worked on their strengths, rather than just their weaknesses. We wanted them to understand that they were there because of what they were good at.'[6]

Even within one team there may well be several sub-units or teams and especially whenever a common goal is not shared or task cohesion is weak. As one example, the bench and the court teams in sports such as basketball may operate to very different agenda and may respond quite differently to successes and failures. So, if you are on the bench and the player that you may replace is having such a great game that you aren't required, how will you feel?

Sport is littered with stories of the tensions between the starting team and the bench, some heavily publicised, others still waiting to be told! Football manager Pep Guardiola has not been slow to remind his entire Manchester City squad what is expected of them, whether or not they make the starting 11:

> They are professionals. When they are not selected they are not happy, after the game they are not happy. But they have to come back happy for the training session. They have to be happy – no other solution. If they are professional they know what it is, the only way to convince their team-mates. If they have bad faces, bad moods or want to show how disappointed they are, they will have a big problem because they are not going to play.[7]

Another part of the solution may lie in underlining the added value the bench may bring to the squad. Renaming *substitutes* as *reinforcements* or *game-changers* is just one practical suggestion we have offered to coaches seeking advice. In international rugby union, Irish players refer to their bench as *the cavalry*, while England rugby manager Eddie Jones refers to his replacements as *the finishers*. Whatever your match-day and pitch-side team routines, the key is to try and reaffirm that so-called *subs* are not subordinates!

Yet, even *within* a starting team there may be different dynamics depending on each position and role. Within a rugby team, for example, the climate that is needed to bring out the best in the backs and forwards may differ. Forwards must work together as a collective while backs may be given more space for creativity and flair.

In a related way, the extent of each players' *role clarity*, or how well-defined their job is within the team, will have a different impact on performance depending on the position in question. With defensive roles, role clarity will usually relate positively to performance. In other words, you need to know what to do and how to do it in order to perform as part of an organised and effective unit. By contrast, attacking roles may suggest a negative relationship between role clarity and performance where too much clarity may actually stifle creativity and flair. In other words being told precisely what you have to do is unlikely to help you find that elusive key for unlocking a resolute defence. So, a reflection on roles and role clarity cannot ignore group dynamics and must take into account factors including playing position, as well as the players' temperaments.

With this in mind, you can see why so many players who managers would describe as 'difficult' are often those in positions where role conflict goes hand in hand with creativity and good performance. The football legend George Best is one example of a creative, attacking genius who ran rings around not only defenders but also team managers, with equal dexterity.

The team in its place

Having developed a profile of the team, the next step is to consider the circumstances in which the team performs. These include the demands made by a particular sport and also the environment in which the team competes. The following three questions may help you understand these issues.

First, does the sport involve activity that is *unitary* (where the task cannot be broken down and where group members typically work together on a single task, e.g. a rowing eight) or is it *divisible* (where the task can be broken down to smaller units and where each team member can be assigned to particular tasks, e.g. a horse riding team or sailing crew)?

Second, how important is either *quantity* or *quality* of contribution to team performance? Some sports emphasise quantity of contribution (often known as *maximisation* tasks, e.g. tug-of-war) while some focus on quality (*optimisation* tasks, e.g. snooker, darts, shooting, archery, golf). Very generally, the former usually involve gross motor skills whereas the latter depend on fine motor coordination. In reality, every sport combines the two, to some degree, but being sensitive to the quantity/quality ratio in your sport can be helpful in deciding the climate or atmosphere that will maximise the chances of team success.

Third, does the team performance depend on what is called 'interaction' or 'co-action'? On the one hand there are *interactive sports* that require coordination between team members (e.g. football, rugby, netball, basketball, hockey) while on the other hand there are *co-active sports* that involve team members performing individually – but in a team context (e.g. golf, bowls, archery, skiing, shooting, darts, snooker). Very few sports are exclusively just one or the other. Instead almost all sports combine unique interactive and co-active elements through different phases of play. Sports such as baseball or cricket are intriguing in this way as both demand high levels of both co-action and interaction. For example, fielding in cricket is principally an interactive team activity but batting and bowling are primarily, but not exclusively, co-active.

Bearing in mind this complex mix between the individual and the collective, it is probably no coincidence that certain players in both baseball and cricket have been renowned as exceptional individual performers – but not great team players. To illustrate, the following extract is taken from the official English cricket website describing one of the greatest English batsmen of all times, Geoffrey Boycott:

> As opener he saw his first task as scoring heavily enough to protect his teams against defeat, and in Test cricket and the County Championship – the matches that counted in the first-class averages – he was as sparing with the attacking strokes as, in retirement, he is strident in his opinions on the game. How valuable he was to England is shown by the fact that only 20 of his 108 Tests ended in defeat, mainly when he failed. . . . A loner, and an insatiable net-player, he was short of friends inside the game; indeed there were many who heartily disliked him because of his selfcentredness.[8]

Boycott may not have won many fans as a team player but as a batsman he was second to none and his contribution to England's team performance was immense.

As sports differ so widely in their nature it is inevitable that the significance of team factors in determining success will also vary. Not surprisingly, the more that a sport requires team members to interact (*interactive sports*) then the more significant team cohesion is likely to be. In sports where athletes may represent the same team but individual performance does not depend on teamwork (*co-acting sports*) then cohesion will be less significant. Some sports may be both highly interactive and co-active (e.g. rowing, tug-of-war) whereas some may be highly interactive but involve less identifiable co-action (e.g. volleyball). Others may be low on both dimensions (e.g. marathon running) and yet others may be co-active but not interactive (e.g. archery, bowls).

Reflecting on all three questions in combination it becomes apparent that the team atmosphere which will maximise performance will vary dramatically between sports. Never imagine that there is a simple formula for team success or that the formula for a winning team remains constant. Instead, at any moment the team character must reflect the particular demands of the situation and the key to success will often lie in identifying or profiling the circumstance and then tailoring the team to these demands.

Successful teams: fit for purpose

To summarise what we have said so far, there is no such thing as a 'good' team – but there are teams that are *fit for purpose*. In other words they are equipped to meet the demands of their particular sport and the challenges that come their way. As a broad foundation for success, a team that is fit for purpose should aspire to create an environment where individual players can flourish and express their individual talents, and where the team's performance becomes greater than the sum of its parts.

It is here that good team management becomes critical (see *Step six*). In a nutshell, successful management is not just about setting and reaching *performance* targets but also involves nurturing *satisfaction* with the team process or dynamic. Short-term performance is important (and in many professional sports is the only guarantee of continued employment for a manager) but without an extra '*value-added*' factor longer-term loyalty and performance will suffer. Most well-managed teams have a healthy balance between attention to team performance and team satisfaction. Let either one of these factors dominate and the team will suffer.

Imagine teams in your chosen sport that have achieved success. Now consider both what they have in common and what makes them different. Very often you will find no common themes or profiles emerging. Each team wil have faced its own distinctive challenges and met these in unique ways. As with the elusive search for a profile of the individual champion, it's not surprising that the team literature has struggled to find a winning team formula. Instead it has been able to identify critical variables that relate to success – and we have outlined these below.

Team cohesion

From an early age we learn to value teams and teamwork. As a consequence we soon develop beliefs about what makes a good team. High on this list is the idea that a tight, cohesive team is a good team and so coaches can come to believe that building a strong *team spirit* is their number one priority. The world of sport constantly echoes and reinforces the significance of team spirit but often in an uncritical way – without taking stock of what this may actually mean, or considering whether or not it can sometimes do more harm than good.

Successful teams will talk about the important role that team spirit has played in their success yet the jury is still out as to which one comes first, spirit or success. Success tends to breed team cohesion – but the impact of cohesion on success is much more debatable. Without doubt, task cohesion is critical – the team that plays and works together is the team that wins together. However, remember that task cohesion and social cohesion are distinct entities, and while one may matter the other may not.

Indeed, healthy conflict and rivalries within a team can often spur that team to success and individual players to want to achieve great things. At times this philosophy has been taken to extremes. Take the example of Leicester Tigers Rugby Club, consistently one of the most successful teams in England and Europe. At their peak in the 2000s, when they won two European championships in successive years (2001, 2002), fights between players would appear to have been commonplace during training, if not actually encouraged:

> The fascinating thing about Leicester is not so much the way they handle big games as how they behave in the privacy of their mid-week practice sessions. The players all have different theories as to why the Tigers are hunting an unprecedented treble tomorrow but it is amazing how often conversation turns to training-ground fisticuffs. Welcome to a club whose idea of perfect harmony is to

ensure players compete from dawn to dusk and, where if necessary, punch one another's lights out.[9]

In the words of a former captain, Martin Corry, these altercations were seen as a healthy sign of commitment, 'They're not something to be proud about but they show that people care. That's the most important thing.'[10]

To effectively marry cohesion with success, our experience would suggest that certain positive steps have to be taken. First, team goals must be clearly defined. Second, expectations of individual players must be high. If goals are unclear and expectations are low or too much emphasis is placed on solidarity at all costs (for example, not showing other players up), then performance will suffer. Third, the focus must rest squarely on task-related issues. Players may be different, with varied social lives and operating in diverse social worlds, and they should be allowed or even encouraged to be different away from the pitch or training ground. Remember, good teams thrive on difference and poor teams stifle individuality. The *value-addedness* of good coaching is that individual strengths are fostered in the service of the team. Needless to say, team competition is when this counts most. A great example of this is US basketball team the San Antonio Spurs. Celebrated for their on-court team play, the talent of individual players has also been recognised. One player who won an NBA All-Star in consecutive seasons with the Spurs (2016 and 2017) once remarked, 'Being close builds chemistry and trust around the team. Then you just go out in the game and you want to fight with your brothers'.[11]

The challenge for team coaches and managers is to create an environment in which individual players flourish while also forging a strong connectedness and sense of team purpose. Commonly, managers and coaches have resorted to elaborate and often exotic team-building enterprises, and the outcomes have not always been pretty!

Building teams – or team building?

For many organisations in sport, as in business, team building has often been seen as the way to go – and especially fashionable *away day* team bonding sessions. According to some commentators, team building enhances loyalty to the team and coach, and harnesses support among team members. Granted, such trips may allow players to become acquainted, but could this have been achieved just as easily, and at a fraction of the cost, in less exotic locations including the training pitch and the changing room? Is the experience likely to achieve longer-term objectives in terms of actually playing together as an effective unit?

Over recent years, many professional sports teams have felt that unless they have been away on the obligatory team-building or bonding holiday before the start of the season – or at the peak phase of competition – then they have missed something out. Why? No one seems to be absolutely sure but since everyone else is doing it, then it has to be right. Apart from financial costs, there are greater potential costs when teams fall out or where different activities occupy players' minds at the expense of forging a unit that plays well together on the pitch and training ground. History shows that in the wrong hands, team building can do more harm than good.

As one extreme example, Leicester City's notorious mid-season 'jolly' to Spain in 2004 springs to mind. The reality was ugly and obscene. Eight players were taken in for questioning by Spanish police following allegations of rape by two women. Four years previously the entire squad had been asked to leave the same Costa del Sol resort because of its anti-social antics.

Some teams have taken the team-building experience to an entirely different plane by replacing the *jolly* with another hackneyed and dangerous message, *No pain, no gain*. Boot camps for teams prior to major tournaments became fashionable in the 1990s. Anecdotal evidence cataloguing the harm and hurt that these experiences have delivered is easy to unearth.

One of the most notorious of these camps was the one used by the South African rugby union team in their disastrous build-up to the 2003 World Cup. This camp involved a whole series of bizarre challenges that are still the stuff of legend. Unfortunately, the consequence of Kamp Staaldraad was lots of pain but very little gain as the Springboks were eliminated in the quarter finals of the competition after a series of under par performances, followed equally swiftly by the resignation of their coach, Rudolph Straeuli. This team-building experience drew interesting criticism from one commentator, 'Many rugby observers also pointed out that trying to eliminate all individuality from a team could be counterproductive, as there are many times during a rugby match when individual initiative can make the difference between victory and defeat.'[12]

More recently, Australian Football team the Adelaide Crows went on a three-day camp with a self-styled 'mind performance company', despite objections by players. What followed was public discord between players and coach, questions about player wellbeing, a reported collapse in team morale and a subsequent performance slump. The camp was followed by three losses in four games, all but ending the Adelaide Crows' 2018 football season.[13]

So, team-building exercises may be a weekend wonder or a financially expensive fiasco. Either way, there can be unforeseen or unwanted consequences. Mind games or slick stunts are not team building. Instead building a team is a skillful, fluid, ongoing process.

Finding the 'I' in TEAM?

As so many proverbs refer to the effects of others on our behaviour it should come as no surprise to learn that we *do* behave differently in the presence of other people than when we are alone. Two experiments dating from the early 1900s first heralded the significance of these effects in sport.

The first compared the times of cyclists who were training either alone, with clubmates or in competition.[14] Norman Triplett found a steady improvement across the three conditions with the poorest times alone and the fastest in competition. In the second study, by Ernst Meumann, the weight that was lifted by men exercising in a training gym when alone was contrasted with the weight they lifted when the author returned to watch them. Consistently their performance improved when being watched, although they were not conscious of the effect.[15]

Social facilitation describes what is happening in both these examples. In simple terms, we work harder in the presence of a team or an audience than when we are alone and especially when we know we are being assessed or evaluated. Later research found that the social facilitation effect was most positive for well-learned, routine tasks but was negative for new or complicated tasks. Which performers are most likely to be adversely affected? No surprises, those who are still learning – novices.

In fact, when others are there the good become better, the bad become worse. This was shown dramatically in an experiment carried out in a pool hall many years ago. Players were secretly rated as being above or below average based on their potting accuracy, and then a group casually stood and watched them play. With an audience those players who were above average improved while those who were below average missed even more.[16]

The implications of these studies are considerable. First, it may be better to insulate athletes from evaluation while they are learning new skills. Second, once the routines are well drilled, it is important to simulate match conditions during training. Otherwise the crowd may later interfere with effective skill execution by athletes. Third, as a team moves forward in a tournament and the likelihood of performing in front of larger crowds increases, it is important to make sure that preparation for each game takes this into account, for example by *stepping-down* (not *stepping-up*) the build-up to each game.

The second social phenomenon worth mentioning is known as *social loafing*. The research evidence here is clear. When we are working in a team, and especially when we know that our individual contribution can't be monitored, then subconsciously we take our foot off the gas or accelerator. A very early experiment in France involved measuring the force exerted by up to six people pulling on a rope and then comparing this with the same people acting in isolation. Time and again in the team situation, individuals only performed at around half what they had shown they were capable of when alone.

Along with personal responsibility, many factors will influence the extent of social loafing including the strength of team identity, the degree of task cohesion and the extent of trust between team members.[17] Once again the implications are considerable. Apart from feedback on team performance, players need *individual feedback* as well. This latter feedback is a constant reminder that each member of the team is being personally monitored. How this feedback is given matters too, as discussed later.

Historically, both social facilitation and social loafing were described separately but over recent years there has been a tendency to describe these team influences together. In summary, the combined effects are as follows.

Summary

Social influences: it all depends!

When the presence of others increases evaluation of a player's performance then easy or well-learned tasks will improve because we are more highly motivated ('social facilitation').

 . . . **but** the execution of more difficult or creative skills may be impaired because of an increase in stress ('social inhibition').

When the presence of others shields us from personal evaluation, performance on easy tasks may become worse because we do not care – especially when goals are not well defined ('social loafing').

 . . . **but** performance on difficult tasks may improve because we are less anxious in a team setting ('social security').

What makes a good team member?

There is clear evidence to suggest that certain individuals are more at home in individual sports while others perform better in a team environment. For some, it is the *collective* that drives them to ever greater heights while for others personal mastery and control through individual achievement is what matters most.

Even within certain sports, such as bowls, tennis or badminton, some players perform at their best in singles competitions while others shine in the team events. In track athletics and swimming, there have been athletes who only ever revealed their true potential in relays as opposed to individual events. One famous example was the 400m runner, Phil Brown, who could always be relied on to produce a spectacular time as part of a very successful GB relay team (e.g. silver medallists in the 1984 Olympic Games) but never came close to matching these achievements in individual events.

Why it is that motivation and performance are influenced in this way is still not clearly understood but almost certainly a number of variables need to be taken into account. Also, it is worth remembering that *performance* and *motivation* are not directly related (see *Step four*), and in fact it may be that a team happens to provide the correct motivational environment for some players to reach their individual zone of optimum functioning (see *Step two*).

In addition, if an athlete is burdened with either a fear of failure or a fear of being evaluated by others (see *Step one*) then the team provides a safer environment in which to perform. A related psychological construct involves *diffusion of responsibility*, or 'a trouble shared is a trouble halved'. Put simply, the burden of expectation may be reduced dramatically when you are one of many in a team. In a similar way, some players welcome the freedom provided by *coming in off the bench* in a team sport. Again, it may be that fear of failure is lowered and so inhibitions are reduced.

In fact, bringing in a replacement just before a match starts may have the same effect for some players. In the 2013 All-Ireland Hurling Final, Clare debutant Shane O'Donnell was only told two hours before the match that he would be on the starting team. In previous games, the 19-year-old forward had experienced acute pre-match anxiety. Yet O'Donnell excelled in the final, scoring 12 points (three goals and three points) from nine touches of the ball. His remarkable hat-trick of goals all came in the first half and helped to secure his team's victory. In a post-match interview, O'Donnell said his last minute introduction to the first team helped him perform, 'I was told close enough to the game so I wasn't too nervous. I didn't have time to get tight about it. I was just excited to get out.'[18]

A second factor to bear in mind is the culture or even society that provides the backcloth for the team. One way in which cultures have been categorised is along the dimension of *collectivism–individualism*. Certain societies place a high value on individualism (most obviously the US) while other countries (most obviously former Eastern bloc countries such as China) have tended to place a greater emphasis on collective action over and above individual ambition.

Players from collective cultures may find themselves more at ease and inspired in team events while those from societies that value individualism may struggle with the competing motives of the individual and the collective. Golf's biennial Ryder Cup competition between the US and Europe provides a fascinating glimpse into such matters. So often the American star players often seem ill at ease with the team basis of the competition while many of the European golfers genuinely seem to welcome and thrive in this environment, relishing the experience as refreshing and different from the daily grind of the professional tour. In the aftermath of Europe's 17.5 to 10.5 defeat of the US in the 2018 Ryder Cup, a golf correspondent remarked that, 'the European team is just that, a team. And a great team at that. Which is why they've won 12 of the last 17 of these Ryder Cups.'[19]

Those who value collectivism may argue that personal ambition is the eighth deadly sin while collective ambition is one of the noblest of human virtues. This may be an exaggeration but without doubt the inspiration of team success does not burn as deeply in some sportspeople as in others. An acknowledgement of this fact can go a long way towards helping establish a motivational climate that will work for a diverse group of players, whatever their sources of motivation, personal or team.

The third question to consider is: what qualities are we looking for in team players? The answer to this question is deceptively easy – individuals. Good teams are not made up of clones or robots who are not allowed to be themselves. Instead, there is a need to strike a very delicate balance – creating an environment that values individuality but one that is bound in a team context where individual goals can still matter yet not as much as the team's. Individual ambition may be important but in a good team it should never be allowed to stand in the way of the collective.

Teams should be constructed and managed primarily to provide an environment where individual talent can flourish and where the collective can become greater than the sum of its parts. As Phil Jackson, former coach of the Chicago Bulls basketball team (six times NBA champions) put it, 'Good teams become great ones when the members trust each other enough to surrender the "me" for the "we".'[20] This hints at a factor which imbues all great teams – a strong, shared identity in which players trust.

Team identity

Research confirms the common sense view that a strong sense of identity (i.e. knowing who you are and what you are about) is closely tied to positive feelings of group solidarity, self-esteem and confidence. Many sport teams ignore this simple message at their cost. For example, instead of building a team around a strong sense of who or what they are, the temptation can be to *borrow* an identity from another team, club or nation, or to rely on history repeating itself in the club colours of old. In these circumstances, history can become a burden and especially where the new team differs in critical ways from its predecessors, including its style of play.

According to one commentator, Sid Lowe, a long established, powerful and positive sense of identity is the defining characteristic of one of the greatest football teams of modern times, Barcelona FC (Barça). After a victory over Real Madrid in one of their famous Clasico games, Lowe wrote:

> Barça's coach, Pep Guardiola, praised his side because even when they trailed, even when they doubted, they remained faithful to their philosophy, their identity. They have one. When it comes to the Clasico, Madrid still do not. Maybe that is the greatest difference of all.[21]

While history can help to instil a sense of belonging, each team has to forge its own identity, and the nature of this identity must be tailored to the characteristics of that group of people and be made clear and obvious to all. But how can this be achieved? One simple technique is to ask the team and management collectively to come up with a number of short words that define what the team is, and to use these words as a constant reminder through the good times as well as the not so good.

In a similar fashion, visual or non-verbal communication may help to reinforce a shared sense of identity. Perhaps the most famous example is the pre-match 'Haka' by the New Zealand All Blacks. Nowadays instantly recognisable, that wasn't always the case. Linked to native Maori culture, some All Blacks players of European ethnicity didn't understand the meaning of the Haka. It was former captain Wayne 'Buck' Shelford who challenged his team-mates, 'If we're going to do it, we're going to do it right . . . perform the Haka properly or not at all. Vote on it.'[22]

Team members agreed to learn the meaning and the movements of the Haka and first performed the 'Haka Mate' in 1985 when New Zealand played Wales in Cardiff. This also reveals another feature of team identity – for it to unify and energise individual players, it must be authentic, come from within and have meaning.[23]

Creating a sense of identity that is real and powerful is not difficult but timing is critical to the enterprise. If a sense of identity comes too soon in a team's development, there may be confusion over what the team actually is. If it comes too late, the team may have already defined itself in a way that will not necessarily improve or sustain a healthy level of performance.

Another common identity problem encountered with many teams is that the team defines itself not by what it is but by what it *isn't*, or by what it thinks it *ought to be*. A practical consequence can be that the team will then play *reactively* rather than *proactively*. Put another way, they wait to see how the opposition plays rather than dictating terms and stamping their own mark on the game. In preparation for competition this tendency may extend to focusing attention exclusively on ways of countering the opposition, instead of playing your own game.

Clearly, match preparation must involve both the reactive and the proactive but without a strong and positive sense of identity then there is a danger that play reverts to planning how to avoid defeat instead of how to win, and preparing for failure reaps its due reward, failure. Interestingly, according to several of his former players, in his team talks Brian Clough, one of England's most successful if enigmatic football managers, always attached far greater importance to his own team's play rather than ways of countering the opposition:

> I worked, taught, coached, cajoled – call it what you want – all with the aim of getting the most out of my lot because, provided I achieved that, I knew that the opposition would have too much on their plate to surprise us.[24]

Although in different sports in different eras, Clough's philosophy resonates with the *strengths-based* approach of New Zealand rugby coach Wayne Smith, as highlighted earlier.

Team continuity and maturity

Any group or team will take time to develop into an effective working unit. Research consistently shows a positive relationship between the length of time that a team plays together and its level of success – but only up to a point. Beyond that point, the climate that has developed in the team will influence whether the team continues to hunger for success or whether it starts to lose its cutting edge.

In the 1960s, an American psychologist called Bruce Tuckman unwittingly laid a false trail when he described group development as a series of orderly stages.[25] According to his model, the group initially gets together and works through the formal 'get to know you' stage (*forming*). Next, there may be heightened tension associated with competition for status and influence in the team (*storming*), before things settle down as norms, rules and standards of behaviour eventually stabilise (*norming*). Finally he argued that the group will have matured to a stage where it can work together as a unit (*performing*) and will continue to perform consistently until members finally decide to go their separate ways (*adjourning*).

Clearly this process all takes time, and when players change, any group or team has to work through the process afresh and performance will invariably suffer during this period of readjustment. However, what the model fails to consider is what happens *beyond* very early stages of development – what climate will help a team to continue to perform well in the medium to long term, in other words, beyond the stage of norming?

Waving not drowning: positive conflict

At this stage, we need to introduce another concept – *waving*. To explain, research suggests a stable team can become lazy or complacent and in these circumstances, team maturity and continuity can lead to underperformance. *Waving* is about allowing healthy levels of conflict to ebb and flow in the team within defined limits. Knowing when to heat things up (*thawing*) and cool things down (*freezing*) is critical in developing the long-term health of the team but has often been ignored, at considerable cost.

In the world of team sports, conflict itself should never be thought of as a dirty word but as an essential ingredient in a healthy team. In this way conflict should never be avoided but must be *managed* effectively (see *Step six*). Teams that function most positively are not those where everyone is going around continually supporting each other, patting each other on the back and discouraging dissent and nonconformity. Research shows that the most stable and productive teams are those where there is a healthy level of rivalry or conflict, where players can feel they can express their own opinions, where they can honestly and openly disagree with others, and where they have space to test their individual potential.

In contrast, the worst teams, whether in sport or business, are usually those that try to eliminate conflict. In such situations, where disagreement is avoided at all costs, a phenomenon known as *groupthink* can easily develop. Groupthink, or a strong tendency to seek agreement, characterises groups where everyone gets on and where everyone strives hard to be like the others and agree with everyone else.[26] Teams that suffer from groupthink underperform and actively go out of their way to suppress difference and individual flair. Worse still, risks or problems may be overlooked or ignored because of groupthink. This is something which is increasingly a concern in preparing teams for missions into space. Training for space travel places a premium on team cohesion. However, in the 1986 Challenger disaster, 'a serious flaw in the decision-making process leading up to the launch', was partly explained by groupthink, and resulted in the death of all seven astronauts.[27]

Teams that avoid groupthink become comfortable with managed conflict and healthy rivalry between team members in an environment where people can be true to themselves without fear of being outlawed. This lesson extends to management and players alike.

Understanding conflict

As outlined earlier in the context of team dynamics, conflict is not a dirty word. Healthy conflict or competition is a necessary ingredient in the make-up of any successful team, but it will often require careful consideration. Before jumping in to deal with a conflict situation, a necessary first step is to spend time reflecting on the nature of the conflict and then deciding how to respond (see *Step six*). When dealing with a conflict, either brewing or brewed, the following questions may help you understand what is going on.

1. Is the conflict genuine or false?

Is this a genuine disagreement between two or more people or is the conflict nothing more than a misunderstanding or communication breakdown. If it is the latter, then the fix is usually more straightforward and involves correcting misperceptions and bridging the communication gap before things go from bad to worse. However, if the breakdown in communication is merely symptomatic of a wider problem within the team then this must be addressed at source.

2. Is the conflict positive or negative?

Many conflicts within teams or between coaches and athletes are positive, reflecting genuine differences of opinion, and these should be acknowledged and worked through. Unfortunately unless these are sorted quickly there is the potential for spillage into other issues, and relationships can become damaged. At the same time, *positive* conflicts may not need to be managed at all but actively encouraged – because they can create a climate that is productive and successful. Deciding the nature of the conflict, positive or negative, will help to determine the nature of the intervention required, if any.

3. Who is involved?

Determining who the key players are is always important in conflict situations. For example, a major dispute within a club may have been sparked by a disagreement between two players but others then become caught up, sometimes against their will. These innocent bystanders soon find there is no fence to sit on but are asked to take sides. Determining who are the main protagonists and who are the support artists is essential in order to effect a long-term resolution.

4. What are the issues?

Often the history of the conflict will reveal an interesting sequence of events involving the interplay between many factors and including the following sources of conflict.

Summary

Sources of conflict

Interests (what I want, what you want)
Understanding (what I understand, what you understand)
Values (what is important to me, what is important to you)
Styles (the way I do things, the way you do things)
Opinions (what I think, what you think)
Identities (who I am, who you are)

Over time, the root cause of the conflict may have been lost or clouded by later events. Unpicking the conflict and its history can be helpful in sequencing resolution techniques. Often this involves dealing with the easiest issues first before moving on to tackle the major bones of contention.

Ordinarily, only one of the factors outlined earlier presents itself as a major obstacle to resolution – and that is *values*. Where one or more players subscribe to a set of values that are out of kilter with the team or club then drastic measures may be called for in order to remedy the problem. If the conflict is based on any of the others then the solution is often easier to reach through a managed process of reconciliation.

5. Who is best placed to deal with this and how?

Having taken time to work through the essential elements, the last stage involves coming up with a strategy for conflict resolution based on one or more conflict management styles (see *Step six*). It may be that you decide to allow the situation to continue, perhaps if the emotional temperature is still not high enough to guarantee engagement, or you may decide that it is better dealt with by others. Whatever decision you reach it must be a strategic one, not influenced by emotion, in order to increase the likelihood of success.

Overcoming obstacles

In this section, we look at a few common problems that those journeying through sport can encounter. We have tried to offer not only a diagnosis of what these obstacles are but, more importantly, how they can be overcome.

'We're slow starters'

This statement may characterise teams that are not entirely sure of themselves – so they wait for the game to spark them into action, when instead they could be far more proactive than reactive. Often teams that wait for a catalyst such as a setback or a bad decision to spur them to action have developed this reactive approach because they have spent too long dwelling on how to counter the opposition instead of how to stamp their mark on the game. In these situations there may be a need to instil a greater sense of identity and hunger based on longer-term goals, and to ensure that the team shares a common sense of purpose. Practical pre-match techniques such as focusing all attention on the first five minutes ('big five') can help.

'We're poor finishers'

This can often reflect on one of two issues – either the team lacks self-belief and its capacity to win through, or the team has too much self-belief and eases up, because it thinks the contest is over. In the first case, it could be that the team is not entirely sure what it is about (e.g. Does it know what its strengths or 'weapons' are?) and how to win. When the chips are down there may be a lack of confidence in the game plan or winning formula for the team as a whole and so players may start to revert to their own ways of doing things. Reinforcing team strategies and game plans can overcome this problem, and using previous occasions where the team won through will help to bolster confidence. However, if the problem is more deep-seated then it may be time to reflect on more radical measures involving the make-up, and shake-up, of the team.

At the other extreme, a team that is too confident may expect that the game will eventually drift its way, rather than devising strategies to take control and move play in its direction. Again, these problems may call for radical solutions involving changes to personnel in order to alter the culture of the team, or strategies can be devised to remind the team how to take charge.

'We drift in and out of games'

As with individual players, where a team plays in fits and starts, individually and collectively, it may be useful to break the game down into much smaller units, and to make sure that evaluation looks across all aspects of the game and not just the last few minutes. Also, with 'drifting' teams, it is helpful to set an objective before the game – such as for each player to focus on the here-and-now and make a big effort to win his or her individual battle with opponents – and for the team to win each half.

'We seem to leave it all on the training pitch'

When teams seem to play better in practice than in competition, an obvious question arises. Have players developed the right preparation techniques to control their own stress levels or has this been left to chance? Are training routines artificial or have they been designed to simulate match conditions? (See also *Step two* for some suggestions about simulating some common distractions in practice situations.) Are players being asked to consider the big picture too much, or are they given freedom only to think of their own task – for example, the player who is their immediate opponent? There should be no reason why training performances cannot be replicated during competition and a systematic review of obstacles to this objective should be undertaken. There may be broader issues, however, in terms of personal motivations and time should be spent understanding these problems.

'We just haven't gelled as a unit'

If a team seems to lack any obvious sense of identity or cohesion, it may be that sufficient time has not been spent buying into a common goal, or there may be different values or agendas at work within the team. Before proceeding, it is important to make sure that task cohesion is really the issue, or do you play well together but simply choose not to mix away from your sport? Has money or other rewards got in the way? Do you know who you are? Have you forged an identity? One remedy may be to use a few key buzz words to remind the team who you are and what you are about (one example is 'BLAH' – buzzing, light, angry, honest).

'We always seem to fall at the critical hurdle'

The team that does well in early rounds of competitions but folds when it comes to the crunch game may be carrying too much baggage around with them. For example, are they burdened by the history of the club or carrying the weight of expectation because of previous failures? In these circumstances there may be a need to cocoon the team from the wider club and supporters, to define the identity from within the group of players and not by external forces or history.

Another technique is to describe a championship campaign as a series of hurdles to be overcome, each one essentially the same but with unique characteristics. A good team meets the last hurdle just like it did the first, and it has in place pre-match routines that never vary. So when the big games do come along, they are just another day – same task, just different venue and opposition. With this in mind, to avoid 'overheating' it is important not to change routines in later rounds of a competition but to consolidate them over time and as a tournament progresses.

Notes

1. Wooden, J. (with S. Jamison) (2007). *The Essential Wooden: A Lifetime of Lessons on Leaders and Leadership*. New York: McGraw-Hill.
2. Psychologist Mourinho inspires with group therapy. *The Sunday Times* (Sport), 1 April 2007, p. 2.
3. MacArthur targeting new challenge. *BBC* (Sailing), 8 February 2005. http://news.bbc.co.uk/sport1/hi/other_sports/sailing/4246831.stm
4. Malam, C. (2018). Mercedes are the best team in ANY sport EVER – Sensational Lewis Hamilton claim. *Express*, 14 March. www.express.co.uk/sport/f1-autosport/931806/Mercedes-Lewis-Hamilton-F1
5. Forsyth, D. (2010). *Group Dynamics* (5th ed.). Belmont, CA: Wadsworth.
6. Hodge, K., Henry, G., & Smith, W. (2014). A case study of excellence in elite sport: Motivational climate in a world champion team. *The Sport Psychologist*, 28, 60–74.
7. Whittell, I. (2018). Pep Guardiola warns Man City squad they 'have to be happy' with competition for places as Kevin De Bruyne return. *The Telegraph*, 26 October. www.telegraph.co.uk/football/2018/10/26/pep-guardiola-warns-man-city-squad-have-happy-competition-places/
8. See http://content-uk.cricinfo.com/ci/content/player/9187.html
9. Kitson, R. (2007). Welcome to Leicester where a punch from the captain is just a sign that you've arrived. *The Guardian*, 19 May, p. 35. Retrieved from http://is.gd/RtqbrZ
10. Ibid.
11. NBA (2014). *Spurs Teamwork* [online video]. Available at: https://m.youtube.com/watch?v=XvW6iUC-Z_Y
12. http://en.wikipedia.org/wiki/Kamp_Staaldraad

13. McClure, S. (2018). Crows camp crisis: Pyke ignored players wishes with Collective Mind. *The Age*, 27 August. www.theage.com.au/sport/afl/crows-camp-crisis-pyke-ignored-players-wishes-with-collective-mind-20180827-p5003j.html
14. Triplett, N. (1897). The dynamogenic factors in pacemaking and competition. *American Journal of Psychology*, 9, 505–523.
15. Lavallee, D., Moran, A., Kremer, J., & Williams, A. M. (2012). *Sport Psychology Contemporary Themes* (2nd ed.). London: Palgrave MacMillian.
16. Michaels, J. W., Blommel, J. M., Brocato, R. M., Linkous, R. A., & Rowe, J. S. (1982). Social facilitation and inhibition in a natural setting. *Replications in Social Psychology*, 2, 21–24.
17. Lavallee, D., Moran, A., Kremer, J., & Williams, A. M. (2012). *Sport Psychology Contemporary Themes* (2nd ed.). London: Palgrave MacMillian.
18. Clerkin, M. (2013). The hurler with the boyband looks, Shane O'Donnell was Clare's hero against Cork. *The Irish Times*, 30 September. www.irishtimes.com/sport/gaelic-games/hurling/the-hurler-with-the-boyband-looks-shane-o-donnell-was-clare-s-hero-against-cork-1.1544064
19. Sagebiel, N. (2018). 2018 Ryder Cup: Team USA still lacks team mindset. *Golf Discount*, October 1. www.golfdiscount.com/blog/news/2018-ryder-cup-team-lacks-team-mindset/
20. Cited in Hodge, K. (2000). *Sports Thoughts*. Auckland, New Zealand: Reed.
21. Lowe, S. (2011). Jose Mourinho's Real Madrid devoid of identity against Barcelona. *The Guardian*, 11 December. www.theguardian.com/football/2011/dec/11/jose-mourinho-real-madrid-barcelona
22. Buck Shelford leads . . . the All Blacks Haka revival. *Rotorua Travel Secrets*. www.rotorua-travel-secrets.com/all-blacks-haka.html
23. Bills, P. (2018). The Jersey: The All Blacks: The Secrets Behind the World's Most Successful Team. London: Pan MacMillan.
24. Clough, B. (with J. Sadler). (2002). *Cloughie: Walking on Water*. London: Headline.
25. Tuckman, B. (1965). Development sequence in small groups. *Psychological Bulletin*, 63, 384–399.
26. Baron, R. S. (2005). So right it's wrong: Groupthink and the ubiquitous nature of polarized group decision making. In M. P. Zanna (Ed.), *Advances in Experimental Social Psychology* (Vol. 37, pp. 219–253). San Diego, CA. Elsevier Academic Press.
27. Teitel, A. S. (2018). How groupthink led to 7 lives lost in the Challenger explosion. *History.com*, 25 January. www.history.com/news/how-the-challenger-disaster-changed-nasa

6 | Your guides

As we explained right at the start of the book, the primary aim of *Pure Sport* is to help you realise your sporting potential. To achieve this objective will involve you eventually taking charge of your own sporting destiny but this can only happen when you have been equipped with the right mental skills to deal with each twist and turn in the road. With this in mind, while the need for help or guidance should hopefully diminish over time, it would be foolhardy, even arrogant, to begin your journey without the services of a trusted guide.

These guides can come in many shapes and sizes, be they coaches, managers, teachers or parents, and it is these folk who are the primary audience for this, the last step in our book. If nothing else this will ensure that the messages which are delivered by coaches are in harmony with those that resonate throughout *Pure Sport*.

For those readers who do not presently see themselves in guiding roles, you may be under-estimating yourself – or what may lie in store for you in the future. It may be that down the way your focus shifts from *doing* or performing to *teaching* or coaching. This is a well trodden path for a great many of those who truly love their sport, and who maybe choose to give something back when their playing days have finally come to an end.

Do also remember that the prinicple of guiding can extend to many positions of responsibility within clubs and teams for those who are still active, including roles such as captain or vice-captain. In this way the material contained in *Step six* should not be seen as the exclusive preserve of those who have already hung up their boots but for anyone who takes charge or guides others in sport.

Ten steps to sporting leadership

When it comes to the science (or maybe art?) of leadership and coaching in sport, there is little point in bombarding you with theory. Both sport and industrial psychology are littered with literally dozens of leadership theories and models. While each may have a different focus and vocabulary, all acknowledge that there is no magic formula for predicting who will make a good leader – and no one style that will be successful across a range of situations. Instead, sports coaches, managers or captains must develop the ability to assess changing situations and use a style which is in keeping with circumstance. In other words, using an approach that meets the needs of others *and* the demands of the situation. Good leadership is not an off-the-shelf formula but having sifted through the research literature, we have identified ten qualities that we have found are often associated with successful leadership in sport.

1. Managing conflict

As we discussed earlier in *Step five*, good leaders are usually good conflict managers: the two go hand in hand. In turn, understanding the source of conflict is often key to developing an appropriate management response. Good leadership can normally succeed in turning conflict situations around using common sense along with structured decision making that avoids an emotional or 'knee jerk' response. Managers or coaches in sport will already be dealing with conflict on a daily basis, and often very effectively. This guidance may simply reinforce your existing good practices or it may help prevent turning a drama into a crisis.

Once you understand the source of conflict, you are better placed to apply the conflict management style that is appropriate for that situation. The literature tends to agree that up to five styles can be used individually or in combination and these are outlined briefly in the following box. Common sense will often dictate which style to employ but even recognising that there are alternatives is helpful, and also acknowledging that we are each inclined to use one style more often than others. If you are interested in finding out which styles you tend to use most often then try the following web link: www.kilmanndiagnos tics.com/catalog/thomas-kilmann-conflict-modeinstrument

Summary

Conflict management styles

Forcing (competing)

When to use: Whenever quick, decisive action is vital and espe-cially on important issues where unpopular courses of action need to be implemented fast – e.g. enforcing unpopular rules, disci-pline, health and safety. It is also a useful style to use on vital issues when you know you are right. Finally, bullies often need to be bullied, otherwise they may try to abuse power or take advantage of you.

Confronting (collaborating)

When to use: This style helps find an integration solution when both sets of concerns are too important to be compromised or when your goal is to learn. It is also useful for merging insights, thereby gaining commitment by incorporating inputs into a joint decision. If hard feelings have been disturbed in a relationship then this style will help to rebuild bridges.

Sharing (compromising)

When to use: Compromising will work best when goals are not too important or worth the effort or potential disruption of more assertive modes. In particular this is true when two opponents with equal power are strongly committed to mutually exclu-sive goals. The style will help achieve temporary settlements to complex issues under time pressure or as a fallback when collaboration or competition fails to be successful.

Withdrawing (avoiding)

When to use: When an issue is trivial, of only passing importance or when other more important issues are pressing. Equally, when you perceive no chance of satisfying your concerns or the potential damage of confronting outweighs the benefits of its resolution. It helps buy time either when emotions are running high, allowing perspective and composure to be regained, or when the gathering of more information outweighs the advantages of an immediate solution. Finally, there may be situations where others can resolve the conflict more effectively or when the issue seems tangential or symptomatic of another more basic issue.

Smoothing (accommodating)

When to use: Accommodate when you realise privately that you are wrong – it will allow a better position to be heard and will show that you are reasonable. It is especially valuable when the issue is much more important to the other person than to yourself. By giving ground you can build up 'social credits' for later issues which are important to you ('you owe me one') and especially when you make it clear that you have made a tactical decision to adopt this approach. Accommodating preserves harmony in difficult times and, longer term, it aids the development of subordinates by allowing them to learn from their own mistakes – letting go.

In one famous example, Manchester United manager Alex Ferguson decided to buy out the contract of his team captain Roy Keane and to let him go. The decision ended a long-running tension between Keane, his manager and team-mates. Ferguson said his decision was triggered by a post-match video interview in which Keane strongly criticised several younger players on the squad. Expressing his approach to managing conflict with players, Ferguson said, 'If they're affecting the control of you or disrupting the dressing room, you have to make the decision – is it worth it?'[1]

In a recent live interview, the current Northern Ireland football manager Michael O'Neill eloquently explained his approach to managing difficult players. To make the job easier, he first of all placed them into one of four categories – high maintenance, high output; high maintenance, low output; low maintenance, high output; and low maintenance, low output. In other words some players may have required greater investment (high investment) but that time and effort was worth it (high output), while others may have drained available energies (high investment) but did not repay that effort in their performance (low output). And the manager's dream player – low investment, high output.

2. Being fair

This issue speaks for itself. Sport rests on principles of fairness or equity. Without fairness, the activity loses meaning for participants and spectators alike. Equally, it is impossible to continue to motivate and lead in an environment where fairness does not reside as a core value – lose fairness and trust will not be far behind. Ongoing hot debates around, for example, drug abuse in various sports,[2] refereeing decisions and racism in football, starkly reveal the central role that fairness plays in sport – and the strong emotions that are stirred when it is felt that unfairness is abroad.

The former England football captain, John Terry, found himself at the centre of a storm of controversy over alleged racist comments made to another player, Anton Ferdinand, during a game between Chelsea and Queens Park Rangers in October 2011.[3] In particular his future role as England captain was thrown into question. Could he continue to command the respect of England players, both black and white, with the suspicion that his sense of fairness may be questionable? His decision to retire from international football came not long afterwards.

As another example, the recent controversy in Australian cricket regarding alleged ball tampering centred on whether a culture had developed in the sport where the principle of winning at all costs had become so dominant that fair play and ethics had flown right out of the window.[4]

From a management perspective, one technique to ensure that fairness is sustained is to remain always conscious of what is known as *the principle of social exchange*. All social relationships can be thought of as exchanges. We give and we receive, and we continue to invest in a relationship so long as we feel that we have had a return on our investment. What each person defines as a reward or a cost is unique but it is rare to find a healthy relationship where all parties don't feel they have benefited – in other words, the rewards outweigh the costs. Over long-term relationships, we become less conscious of social exchange (*'What did I give, what did I get'*) but in new relationships or when relationships have been damaged, then exchange awareness is heightened (*'Look what I did for them, look what they did/didn't do in return'*). In these situations it is critical that there is sensitivity towards feelings of being treated unfairly when interacting with team members or athletes.

Taking this approach further, leadership itself can be characterised as a process of exchange. Leaders are given status and power but in return those who are being led will expect to be rewarded – with fair treatment and with success. Once more, in the early stages of a relationship there is heightened awareness of costs and benefits, and it is dangerous to make an assumption that all is ok without relying on regular feedback to check your perceptions against those of others.

3. Making good decisions

Moment by moment, successful leadership hinges on making the right decisions at the right time. This could include devising and revising game plans, substitutions, training schedules, team selections or longer-term strategies. Ultimately a coach, manager or captain will be judged by the effectiveness of these decisions. Quite naturally, you could assume that decision making is solely about the *quality* of the decisions made. However, this ignores a second crucial element, *acceptance*, or others' willingness to agree with and then act on that decision. A good decision means nothing if no one listens and it isn't implemented.

The success of an endurance expedition, as an extreme example, will often hinge on the fine balance between decision quality and decision acceptance. Many disasters have occurred because one or both were not taken into account. For examle, on his ill-fated expedition to reach the South Pole, Captain Robert Falcon Scott may have inspired his crew to unimaginable heroics by their uncritical acceptance of his decisions – but what about the quality of those decisions? On the other hand, Captain William Bligh may have been one of the greatest navigators and sailors of the eighteenth century but by failing to match the quality of his decisions with acceptance of those decisions by the crew of his ship, *HMS Bounty*, he created a recipe for mutiny.

Many leaders are strong in either one or the other but rarely excel in both. An exception to the rule, also from the world of polar expeditions, was the Anglo-Irish adventurer Ernest Shackleton (1874–1922). He was a man who combined extraordinary management skills with sound judgement that ensured not only the success of his expeditions but also the safety and well-being of his crew. One of his greatest attributes was his wry sense of humour, as the advertisement for his 1914–1916 *Endurance* expedition clearly shows, 'Men Wanted: For hazardous journey. Small wages, bitter cold, long months of complete darkness, constant danger, safe return doubtful. Honour and recognition in case of success.'[5]

Successfully balancing decision quality with decision acceptance requires the adoption of a range of management styles, along with knowing which of these styles is best suited to which situation. There may be times when decision quality is critical and you are confident in the information available to you, and so you can take a more *directive* line. At other times, when both quality and acceptance are significant, then you may choose to *involve others* to some degree, or where acceptance is the overriding concern then *delegation* may be most successful. Once again, it all depends – and you can depend on the fact that successful managers typically match the right style with the right situation.

On those occasions where you are compelled to make a high quality decision, other techniques can be brought to bear in order to make sure that this decision is not contaminated by unintended biases. In some respects this decision-making technique simply builds on and strengthens what we do normally in combining different bits of information in decision making. We gather the evidence and then assign different levels of importance to each element before deciding on a course of action. Unfortunately unless this process is systematic there is a real danger that personal biases will creep in and certain elements will assume greater significance than they deserve.

To illustrate the technique in practice, imagine that you are a hockey coach selecting a team for an important league game. Many players can be pencilled in without much thought. However, there is one key defensive position where you have to decide between two players. Both players have strengths and weaknesses and it will be potentially divisive within the club unless handled sensitively.

To help decide and also to provide you with a solid justification when the team is announced, you first list all the attributes that are relevant to that position in the forthcoming match. Having listed these factors, you then assign a weight to each factor, from 1 (least important) to 10 (most important).

The two players are then scored on each factor (say out of 10) and their rating is then multiplied by the weighting to produce a score that is then totalled and can be compared, as in the following table.

For this particular position, Player A, with a total score of 393, is chosen over Player B, with a score of 335. Critically, when you now talk to both players you can provide feedback as to why the choice was made and why you believe it was the correct decision. It will also provide the unsuccessful player with feedback that can be translated into positive action for the future. At the end of the day, the player may still not like your decision – but at least they can understand why you made it.

Case study

Selecting fairly					
		PLAYER A		*PLAYER B*	
Attribute	*Weight (W)*	*Rating (R)*	*W × R*	*Rating (R)*	*W × R*
Speed	7	4	28	6	42

Distribution	6	7	42	6	36
Close stick work	4	5	20	3	12
Passing	3	8	24	7	21
Strength	8	9	72	2	16
Tackling	10	3	30	6	60
'Team member'	5	6	30	4	20
Age	2	8	16	4	8
Fitness	7	7	49	5	35
Competitiveness	8	8	64	8	64
Durability	3	6	18	7	21
TOTAL			393		335

4. Motivating

> Coaches who can outline plays on a black board are a dime a dozen. The ones who win get inside their players and motivate (Vince Lombardi).[6]

A good leader must have the capacity to motivate others, but don't imagine that this is a mystical art. It is a *science* that is understandable and applicable. To repeat earlier messages, it is important to recognise that motivation is not just about a list of factors but is a *process*, a process that moves us – that gets us out of bed in the morning just as it spurs an athlete to dig deep into dwindling physical reserves at the end of a gruelling competition.

A useful psychological model for describing the process of motivation has already been outlined in *Step four*.

To be motivated, initially the player must be able to recognise that increasing his or her effort can positively change performance (*Expectancy*), the size of the effect being influenced by *ability* (perceived and actual) and the *role* or position that the person is asked to play. Next, *instrumentality* refers to the player's belief that an improvement in *performance* will reflect in an increase in *rewards*. Without this recognition, it is unlikely that the player will expend effort.

The term *outcome* does not simply refer to concrete rewards or benefits (e.g. trophies, titles, money, status, prestige) but includes intrinsic factors such as a sense of mastery, control, well-being, enjoyment and self-esteem. Too much emphasis on extrinsic rewards can be demotivating in the longer term while intrinsic motivation provides a more solid foundation for ongoing success. Furthermore, it is not absolute reward but what we receive relative to others – am I getting as much or more or less for what I do?

To apply this model successfully in everyday situations, the first step involves really getting to know what makes each one of your players or athletes tick. Only then is it possible to use this framework for understanding individual problems and delivering effective remedies. Perhaps the player feels that outcomes or rewards do not depend on personal performance, that their place is secure or that they will be dropped whatever they do – in other words, their fate is already sealed. Perhaps the player feels undervalued or believes that s/he is not able to improve performance however hard they try? Perhaps the player's personal goals and rewards are no longer the same as those of the team or club, or the outcomes are not clearly defined?

Whatever the case, by systematically applying this model it is possible to pinpoint where the problem lies and to work out a positive way forward. It gives the coach, captain or manager the opportunity to pinpoint what is going on inside each player's head and to understand their priorities, rewards and values – without doubt one of the keystones to successful coaching. As to the practical implications of this model for dealing with players, a number of the most important points are summarised in the following.

Summary

Positive coaching: five principles

1. **Know your players**: You must be aware of the priorities, valued rewards and goals of each player in order to maximise

potential. No two players will have identical value systems and allowance must be made for differences.

2. **Provide positive feedback**: Players must be provided with positive feedback on individual performance to maximise effort on future occasions.

3. **Relate effort to performance**: An individual is only likely to increase effort if there is a belief that this work will actually improve performance. By providing clear feedback on performance, you will improve the effort put into practice.

4. **Relate rewards to performance**: A player or athlete must be made aware that a change in performance will lead to either an increase or decrease in outcomes or rewards (either concrete or 'intrinsic') that are valued.

5. **Be challenge oriented**: By setting challenging but reachable goals and providing clear feedback on attainment, high levels of performance can be maintained. Goals must not be too distant and must be attainable.

5. Reflecting

As the previous point makes clear, a good leader in sport must have the capacity not only to look *outwards* – to devise tactics, to analyse and assess – but also to look *inwards* – to constantly reflect and adjust his or her own behaviour. Fortunately, many of the performance management skills already described earlier are directly transferable to the world of coaching and management.

Performance profiling (discussed in *Step four*) gives you a way of systematically evaluating your strengths and weaknesses as a coach. Goal setting is also important in providing practical techniques for effecting change. In the spirit of *Step four*, the profiling attributes you choose have to be personal but as a starting point you could refer to the checklist in the following box. This was developed spontaneously during a workshop we ran for top-level coaches across many team and individual sports a few years ago. When asked to define the characteristics of a good coach, these skills and characteristics were identified.

It is unlikely you could hope to possess all of these qualities – but knowing what you *can't do* as well as what you *can do* then equips you with the knowledge of which gaps need be filled and how to fill them.

In general terms, psychologically, we are most comfortable and least challenged when we are surrounded by those who are like us and who reinforce our views. Difference is more challenging than similarity but good teams thrive on the challenge of diversity. With this in mind it is critical to have the courage to use people who complement you rather than simply reflect or reinforce you – in other words, those who fill your gaps rather than reinforce your defences. Many of the most successful management teams in sport have been built on this principle – complementarity yet difference. Or put more bluntly, beware the 'yes' men and women!

Summary

Essential coaching qualities: a checklist

Personal qualities	Interpersonal skills	Technical skills	Knowledge
Energetic	Delegator	Goal setter	Sport-specific
Visionary	Effective manager	Analyst	Tactical awareness
Confident	Networker	Counsellor	Biomechanics
Enthusiastic	Listener	Innovator	Physiology
Honest	Communicator	Planner	Psychology
Resilient	Empathiser	Decision-maker	Nutrition
Punctual		Tactician	Political sense
Positive thinker		Administrator	Medical

Self-disciplined	Selector	Knowing when to walk
Committed		Sceptical enquirer
Patient		
Adaptable		
'Personality'		
Stress manager		
Questioning		

6. Adapting

The late football manager Brian Clough was a legend, especially when working in concert with his sidekick, Peter Taylor. Between them they plucked first Derby County and then Nottingham Forest from obscurity to the dizzy heights of national and international league and cup success. Euphemistically, their combined management style is perhaps best described as idiosyncratic, being liberally laced with the capacity to surprise – especially in team preparation techniques.

In one famous example, before Nottingham Forest's victory over Malmo in the 1979 European Cup, Clough passed a crate of beer to his players on the bus that took his team to the stadium before the match! This unconventional idea stemmed from a well-founded belief that players perform best in a relaxed frame of mind, or in his words, 'Nottingham Forest would be represented by good players who were relaxed . . . That's why we had beer on the coach . . . Forest's footballers weren't uptight footballers when they took to the field.'[7]

Along with Peter Taylor, Clough was able to mould both young players and previously discarded older players into formidable teams with a distinctive style of football. On the strength of his proven achievements, Clough alone was invited to take over from Don Revie at Leeds United in 1974.

The Leeds team that Brian Clough inherited was well estab-lished and had achieved incredible success over several years. How-ever, many of the players were seasoned internationals and did not respond well to Clough's unique and directive style of management. Within 44 days the relationship had ended. As he reflected many years afterwards:

> I was confronted by a seething, resentful, spiteful dressing room when I arrived on my first morning . . . Leeds had done it all . . . They weren't threatened, any of them, because they felt they were bigger than me.[8]

A salutary lesson for Brian Clough and for any aspiring team manager – new brooms may sweep clean but they can also be broken in the process.

In that era, Clough and Taylor made a superb management team for aspiring clubs – but that management style did not transfer to the bear pit of Leeds United. The capacity to change and adapt is a core principle of good leadership, and it is a dangerous strategy to assume that reputation alone will allow you to impose a style. It may work but it is a high-risk strategy with no guarantee of success. As Brian Clough later remarked in his autobiography, 'My way – aggressive, blunt and hell-bent on making changes – was never going to work.'[9]

A more sensible approach may be '*softly softly*' – carefully and quietly assess the situation before deciding how best to proceed. Sometimes this may involve going with the existing flow until sufficient credit has accumulated, sometimes imposing your will earlier if the situation is critical. Whatever else, this must be a careful, considered response as opposed to a hasty gut reaction.

In a similar vein, adapting to the changing needs of the team or athlete is critical in continuing to foster a healthy relationship. Sport is littered with stories of successful coach–athlete relationships that have foundered during the *sturm und drang* (storm and strife) of adoles-cence, or even beyond, for no other reason than the coach failed to recognise that the athlete was growing up! The relationship, and the coach, must change or perish in the process.

Research consistently shows that athletes and players look for different types of support and advice at different stages of their careers.[10] For example, young athletes generally need considerable social support early on but this need decreases over time. In addition, too much emphasis on skills training can be de-motivating, even boring, for many young people. Technical advice is often most appropriate in mid-career while more mature athletes will often want personal support to help them through the ups and downs of élite competition.

7. Monitoring

Most of the skills and techniques described in this chapter ask the leader to look *inwards*, to reflect. But introspection must be counterbalanced with an awareness of what is going on *outside*. While the search for personality traits attached to leadership has been disappointing,[11] one attribute that often characterises good leaders is social perception or *social intelligence* (being aware of others and also having the skills to manage human relations, frequently referred to nowadays as emotional intelligence (EI)). More generally, leaders typically are described as being either socio-emotionally oriented (primarily concerned with good relations and maintaining harmony) or task oriented (concerned with the task at hand rather than good relations).

Whichever orientation you favour, it is important that the needs, expectations and feelings of others are accommodated in some way and then are reflected in the range of management styles that you use.

Monitoring team dynamics can alert you to emerging issues, including processes of social influence. As an example, although certain individuals may not have been given formal roles or titles in a team or club, they may still be very influential, and it would be dangerous to ignore the power that these players can wield. Such individuals shouldn't be easily dismissed as disruptive influences or as a threat to authority but instead you should work at how you can harness their influence to the advantage of the team. This requires person-management skills that may not always sit comfortably with you – but the effort will be repaid.

To summarise, three types of awareness should be worked on:

Summary

Coaching awareness

Self-awareness: Become aware of your preferred style of coaching/captaincy and try to then expand and develop the range of approaches that you use.

Social awareness: As with motivation, a recognition of the characteristics of the teams and individuals you are working with is important. Also develop the skill of assessing changing situations quickly and adapting your approach accordingly. Try to balance the time that is spent on either technical skills or interpersonal concerns depending on the demands of the situation.

Exchange awareness: Keep in mind that leadership is a two-way process. Followers only allow themselves to be influenced and led if they receive something in return.

8. Communicating

Reflecting and monitoring mean nothing if the information isn't then communicated effectively. For those new to coaching, management or captaincy, there is bound to be some anxiety about giving team talks and holding team meetings. As a result there is a temptation to fall back on a script or the delivery style of someone you admire. This can be reassuring but experience suggests that finding your own style sooner rather than later is likely to be more effective.

Many of the best coaches and captains were far from great orators, preferring to speak with their actions or with a few, well-chosen words. As one example, Roy Keane (who managed Sunderland to Championship success in his first season in charge of the team, 2006–2007) never expected more than ten minutes attention from his players:

There might be a gut feeling, something that came to me during the week about our own team and our own performance. There might be something I might have heard before, but I try to add my own piece to it. We make players aware of the opposition. Five or 10 minutes of the opposition on DVD and then I talk to them. That's all you have really, 10 minutes.[12]

Traditionally coaches and players alike have placed great store on pre-match talks, supposedly rousing the troops to battle but more likely providing little more than background noise (it is estimated that only around 5 per cent of pre-match talks can be remembered after the game!). Modern changing rooms bear little resemblance to the 'head-banging and hugging' locker rooms of old, with, at long last, an acknowledgement that each player must be given personal responsibility for preparing in a way that works best for him or her.

Equally, half-time tirades have been replaced by more measured use of the available time, often incorporating a *down-time* for players to draw breath and reflect before gathering and sharing information and instruction. When reading about great managers there is often a need to take the headlines with a hefty pinch of salt. For example, consider Alex Ferguson's half-time 'hair dryer' treatment, which has become the stuff of legends. The reality is that this approach was the *exception* rather than the norm. As he reported back in 2008:

> So there are two types of team talk – one if you're doing well and another if you're not. The observations on the first-half are the most important thing. You only have about seven or eight minutes to rectify or resolve the situation if the match isn't going to plan. You should never dodge any issues. I don't know what team talks are like in other dressing-rooms but I try to get to the nub of the problem and solve it as quickly as I can. After that, you have to motivate your players to start the second half. As manager you have to produce the right words and the right volume to make players very aware of their responsibilities and how they can improve.[13]

In truth, it is likely that many of the traditional rants and rituals owe far more to relieving the coach's stress than preparing the players or athletes – and perhaps should be consigned to the waste-bin of history. Also remember that a law of diminishing returns will apply – the first rant may have maximum impact but the second may make less impression, and as for the third, fourth and fifth, who knows . . . ?

Content over style

Communication works best if you employ a style that is your own. However, it is the *content* of the communication rather than its style that is critical to motivating players and to influencing their performance. Through words and deeds, verbal and nonverbal, the coach and captain have the power to establish the climate for the team, a climate that can either allow players to develop or can inhibit expression and the display of skill. In order to maximise impact, here are a few simple communication rules, based on the previous steps:

Summary

Communicating effectively: golden rules

Set goals

The highest levels of attainment will be reached where players are aware of what is expected of them, and where the goals that are set are difficult but possible. Describe performance in relation to objective standards or goals wherever feasible. These goals should be short term, challenging but attainable.

Work to an agenda

Have work schedules already to hand before sessions begin but be flexible enough to allow changes should circumstance demand. Communicate your requirements clearly in terms of training schedules, etc.

Provide positive feedback

Let those individuals who reach these goals know that you are pleased. Positive reinforcement works; negative reinforcement is less effective. Use moderation and avoid lengthy comments. Be objective and avoid references to personalities.

Monitor performance

Ensure that players are aware that you are constantly keeping an eye on their performance, in training and during competitions. This does not imply a constant dialogue but subtle reminders of your vigilance.

Emphasise quality

Through monitoring, place the emphasis on quality of work rather than quantity. Again, feedback is important.

Allow honest mistakes

With the emphasis on positive feedback it is important to allow players the freedom to make 'honest mistakes'. Constant criticism is bound to constrain expression and creativity.

Past experience may inhibit players' acceptance and learning from feedback by a coach. A crucial factor in this is trust. Recent research on communication styles highlights the positive effect of *wise feedback*.[14] This research found individual feedback had a greater effect on performance when it conveyed three related messages: i) you belong in this group; ii) we have especially high standards; and iii) I believe you can achieve our high standards. How a coach speaks and what a coach says must be tailored to each player. With trust and a chance for a player to learn, real improvement is possible.

9. Being passionate: it has to matter

Of all the defining qualities of sporting leaders, there is one that cannot be ignored – *passion*. In other words, it has to matter. Without commitment, a person's capacity to genuinely inspire others will always be questionable. This does not always mean having *charisma* or great skills of oratory but it does have to matter. Some people have taken this quality well beyond the limits, and at such times too much commitment can be as dangerous as too little (see *Step one*).

This brings us to an important question. When all is said and done, does sport really matter that much? After all, in comparison with many things in life, such as illness and death, it is clearly less important. But strangely, having come to terms with the fact it doesn't *really* matter as much as you first thought then it *can* matter all the more because of that honest acknowledgement of the purity of the endeavour – in other words, pure sport. This sense of perspective is a key theme underpinning this book, and one that we have returned to time and time again. You have to care – but not too much.

Not everyone can or should display the raw, unbridled passion of sporting legend. To try to be someone that you are not will take you down an uncomfortable road. Some may prefer the quiet rage while others the ice cool performer. Some others may play the extrovert or even the flamboyant showman. Having managed Barcelona FC to phenomenal success, Pep Guardiola has led Manchester City to the top of the English Premier League. He said that above all else it is not his charisma (he recently described himself as 'boring') but his *work rate* that sets the tone for players:

> I am not a special guy but I am so good at working, working, working a lot and they have to work too. . . . It is impossible to have a season that is perfect. We will have bad moments and we will have to work to overcome them because in the end the players react to what the club is, what the manager and the staff are and, of course, they know we work for them. . . . Now we start again. That's why it is special. It's a new challenge. That's why we stay here. The moment I am not hungry I am leaving.[15]

There is no magic formula but somewhere within you the flame has to continue to burn brightly and when it doesn't, it may be time to let go.

10. Letting go

Many coaches and managers bring extraordinary levels of commitment to their sport, and then assume that all those they work with must also carry the same passion. Passion matters – but then we encounter a paradox. Good leaders must know *how* and *when* to let go. As Zen masters tell us in the martial arts, to gain control you have to know when to give up control.

In any walk of life involving supervision and the nurturing of skills and knowledge, the true sign of a job well done involves letting go or *voluntary redundancy*. The gentle hand on the tiller may never disappear completely but for long periods of the voyage the auto-pilot should become just as effective. Knowing that this end point, *empowerment*, is a happy consequence of good leadership should not be forgotten. Too many leaders find letting go of the reins difficult but any well managed team or athlete must aim to reach a point in their development where the manager, coach or even captain should be prepared to quietly relinquish the driving seat – for stages of the journey at least.

Good leadership

At this stage, let's return to the 64,000 dollar question – what makes a good captain, coach or manager? As you glance back to the earlier parts of the book you will find that we have already posed similar questions, including '*What makes a champion?*', '*What makes the winning mind?*' and '*What makes a winning team?*' It will probably come as no surprise to learn that the answer to the first question will be the same as the rest – it all depends! Good leaders in sport, as elsewhere, come in all shapes and sizes, and so searching for a single formula to explain their success is futile.

To illustrate, take any sport and then list who you would rate as the five outstanding managers or captains. Now briefly sketch the psychological profile of each. Almost certainly you will notice that they differ radically from each other not only in their management styles but also their characters or personalities. Admittedly, there may be some who you like or admire more than others – but in terms of success, a consistent winning formula is hard to spot.

Many of the greatest coaches and managers, and even captains, may not have had great talent as players but were still able to bring superb qualities to team management. Take professional football. Research[16] has shown that of the 26 managers who coached winning teams in the Premiership (formerly the First Division) in England between 1945 and 2000, fewer than one in five had ever won more than six international caps. Remarkably, managers including Bob Paisley and Bill Shankly (both of Liverpool) and Sir Alex Ferguson (Manchester United) were never capped by their native country, Scotland. Similarly, Arsène Wenger (Arsenal) never played for France and José Mourinho was never capped for Portugal. Summing it all up, when asked if it was necessary for a great manager to have been a great player, Arrigo Sacchi (who won two European Cups as manager with AC Milan but had never even played professional football) joked, 'What's the problem here? . . . If you want to be a good jockey, it's not necessary to have been a horse!'[17]

Admittedly, to understand the game and all its intricacies at the highest level may require experience and knowledge of that world but to place excessive emphasis on playing experience alone can be dangerous – and expensive.

Psychologists have spent a great deal of time trying to define what makes a good leader and reluctantly they have concluded that the search is pointless. Instead, attention has turned away from a search for personality types and towards the practical functions that leaders must perform, and the circumstances in which they must operate, which we have explored earlier.

The primary task of good leadership is not to crave fame and glory, to boost one's ego or to exert power and influence for its own sake. Instead the primary function of a coach or manager is to maximise the potential of those you are privileged to lead. To emphasise this point, consider what the former South African President, Nelson Mandela, had to say about leadership, 'It is better to lead from behind and to put others in front, especially when you celebrate victory when nice things occur. You take the front line when there is danger. Then people will appreciate your leadership.'[18]

In the world of sport, some great leaders have loved basking in the spotlight – but some of the greatest have taken their lead from Nelson Mandela. One man who fitted this bill particularly well was the legendary basketball coach John Wooden who died in June 2010 at the age of 99.

John Wooden

John Wooden was raised on a small farm in Indiana from where he went on to gain a scholarship to Purdue University. A reasonably talented yet hugely competitive basketball player himself, he became an All-American college player before turning to coaching at the age of 38. In a remarkable career spanning 27 consecutive years with the UCLA Bruins (1948–1975), he succeeded in catapulting the team from the depths of the Pacific College Conference to the pinnacle of their sport, with an unsurpassed record including 88 consecutive victories, ten NCAA championships (including seven in a row), 38 consecutive NCAA tournament victories and four years where the team went undefeated for the entire season.

The following excerpt, taken from a fan's online tribute, eloquently captures the man – and his many achievements:

> Not too keen on flamboyance, Coach Wooden was a modest man who did not seek the limelight; and at the same time, showed the utmost grace and decency to all UCLA's opponents – win or lose. As for his coaching record, neither an 80.6% winning percentage and winning ten NCAA championships define the man completely. Rather, it is the respect he still garners today from those who are in or simply follow college basketball, which define him best. Undoubtedly, John Wooden was the greatest coach ever in any sport, and is the measuring stick for which all other great coaches of all sports will be measured until the end of time.[19]

How was John Wooden able to bring out the best in those he coached, year after year? The following quotes taken from the man himself begin to reveal the basis of his success. This approach did not rely on cheap tricks or gimmickry but the promotion of a philosophy that meshes very closely with the principles described throughout *Pure Sport*.[20, 21]

Case study

In the words of John Wooden . . .

- Don't let what you *cannot* do interfere with what you *can* do.
- If you're not making mistakes, then you're not doing anything.
- Be more concerned with your character than your reputation, because your character is what you really are, while your reputation is merely what others think you are.
- Do not let either praise or criticism affect you. Let it wash off.
- Ability may get you to the top, but it takes character to keep you there.
- Don't measure yourself by what you have accomplished, but what you should have accomplished with your ability.
- In anything, failure to prepare is preparing to fail.
- Be quick, but don't hurry.
- A player who makes a team great is more valuable than a great player.
- Talent is God-given. Be humble. Fame is man-given. Be grateful. Conceit is self-given. Be careful.

Adding value

Measuring leadership solely by the number of trophies on the shelf can be misleading. A far more useful measure is the principle of 'adding value' as captured by the simple question, '*What talent and resources were available and what was achieved?*' On both counts, John Wooden was exceptional. In the early years, he was able to build a team with limited resources. Beyond that time, he had the management skills and coaching acumen to be able to keep building and rebuilding the team thereby creating a sporting dynasty.

John Wooden did enjoy fame in later life but some of the greatest sports coaches or managers will remain unsung local heroes who, against all odds and with minimum resources, create an environment where potential talent is realised and, in team sports, where the team becomes greater than the sum of its parts.

Equally, inspirational captains are often those who achieve great things but with limited resources, or who mould a team during its formative years – sometimes referred to as *cultural architects*. In truth, the history of sport is littered with examples of those who were later labelled as great captains and coaches but perhaps were nothing more than exceptionally lucky to be linked to a team that had reached its prime – they happened to be in the right place at the right time. This *accidental heroism* contrasts with truly outstanding captains and coaches who were able to lift and inspire their teams to achieve great things from nowhere and against the odds.

In conclusion, in sport as elsewhere, a great deal has been written about what makes a great leader. Reflecting on this literature, it is too easy to stand in awe of those who have been there and done it all, and to feel humbled and inadequate by comparison. Yes, there have been exceptional leaders with remarkable skills throughout the history of sport but equally it is amazing how unremarkable these giants can be when you actually meet them in the flesh! The most striking characteristic they share is that they are comfortable with who they are, they know what they want and they know how to go about getting it.

Rather than placing these individuals on a pedestal, our intention has been to learn from previous triumphs and failures alike, and then to show you in very practical ways the factors you can combine to help you carve out your own unique career in sport management, if that is your choice. The rest is up to you.

Guidebooks

Along with your human guides it may be useful to have access to other sources of information besides *Pure Sport*. Here are a few examples of recent applied sport psychology textbooks that you may find helpful.

Andersen, M. B. (Ed.) (2000). *Doing Sport Psychology*. Champaign, Ill.: Human Kinetics.

Cotterill, S. T. (2018). *The Psychology of Performance*. London: Routledge.

Eubank, M., & Tod, D. (2017). *How to Become a Sport and Exercise Psychologist*. London: Routledge.

Horn, T. S., & Smith, A. (Eds.) (2018). *Advances in Sport and Exercise Psychology* (4th ed). Champaign, Ill.: Human Kinetics.

Kremer, J., Moran, A., Walker, G., & Craig, C. (2012). *Key Concepts in Sport Psychology*. London: Sage.

Lavallee, D., Kremer, J., Moran, A., & Williams, M. (2012). *Sport Psychology: Contemporary Themes* (2nd ed). Houndsmill, Hants: Palgrave Macmillan.

Leavey, G., & Breslin, G. (2019). *Mental Health and Well-Being Interventions in Sport*. London: Routledge.

Moran, A. (2018). *Mental Toughness in Golf*. Series of audiobooks available from Mindcool Productions (www.mindcool.com).

Moran, A., & Toner, J. (2017). *A Critical Introduction to Sport Psychology* (3rd ed). London: Routledge.

Mugford, A., & Cremades, J. G. (2018). *Sport, Exercise, and Performance Psychology*. London: Routledge.

Overcoming obstacles

In this section, we look at a few common problems that those journeying through sport can encounter. We have tried to offer not only a diagnosis of what these obstacles are but, more importantly, how they can be overcome.

'They never seem to follow the game plan'

This is often indicative of different agendas at work within a team and often characterises either young teams (who have never been on message), or mature teams (who have drifted off message). In both situations, it is useful to identify the cliques within the team or among management. Do some players sit together, train together, or do younger and older players not mix? The solution involves gentle social engineering to mix the team up and break alliances, for example by introducing intra-team competition, re-organising changing room arrangements, travel arrangements, accommodation, etc.

'They lack flair and only do what they're told'

This may be a consequence of being too 'hands on' – whatever instructions have been given in the past have worked so why bother thinking when you just do what you are told? This can be a hard nut to crack but has to begin with an honest acceptance that a culture of dependency has been fostered and it is now start-ing to have an adverse effect on performance. For example, play-ers may turn up for games expecting to be motivated by someone else. What walks into the changing room is more important than what walks out, and danger lies in placing too much emphasis on that short time in the changing room prior to games. Inspira-tional team talks may work occasionally and exceptionally but it is impossible for even the most eloquent coach or manager to have the same impact time after time. Instead, it is likely that a law of diminishing returns will apply – and the rest will become history!

'They're a very quiet team'

Quietness can signify two things – either a team that knows what it is about and so has no need to talk, or a team that lacks the self-belief to express itself. Which explanation is more accurate in any given case must be worked through, to find out if there is actually a problem or not. The answer lies in having a level of communication that does not ebb and flow as the tide of a game changes but is used to manage the game and the impression created. For example, if the team becomes quiet when the tide is flowing against them this is quickly picked up by the opposition as a sign of a lack of confidence.

Beforehand, it may be useful to designate key players with the responsibility to keep the 'noise level' at the right pitch across the pitch. Positions such as goalkeeper are crucial in this regard along with key players in specific areas (e.g. defence, midfield, attack). Also, bench players can be given specific responsibility for keeping the volume high. At the same time you should also consider whether there is a more deep-seated problem of management's making – they don't talk because they don't have anything to say. In other words, they are merely acting to your instructions. The remedy does not need repeating – learn to let go.

'It's a lazy team'

Labelling any team as 'lazy' without sufficient evidence is a big mistake. However, if it becomes apparent that certain team members are not working hard enough, perhaps the label is justified. Laziness can occur in a team that has achieved too much too soon and is finding it difficult to re-energise, or a team that has set its sights too low, or a team that has become too tight or too cohesive. In each case, the solution must involve ways of shattering the collective comfort zone, piece by piece. Unexpected changes in personnel may often be called for to stem the drift towards mediocrity but often drastic action is the only real cure.

'There are one or two in the squad who just aren't team players'

In any team there will always be those who do not appear to pull in the same direction as everyone else. Dealing with these players can be very difficult and time consuming, especially when their individual talent is considerable. Eventually, there is no alternative other than to sit down with a cost/benefit balance sheet and calculate the pros and cons – i.e. what does the player *cost* in terms of collective action and what does he or she *give* in personal performance? On the basis of this analysis, hard decisions must be made but do not be fooled into assuming that yet more attention will be the solution. Further attention often simply rewards attention-seeking behaviour, and at the same time sends the wrong signal to other players. Often, the harder you try the easier it will be for the player to keep running away.

'How can I get my subs to make an impact?'

Increasingly, coaches and managers are becoming interested in practical ways of ensuring that their substitutes are as alert and focused as possible while they wait to be called into action in the match. This is a difficult challenge because it's hard to keep players' minds active when they're sitting on the bench. In general, however, it's helpful to ask players to look for certain patterns of play arising in their position and to encourage them to warm-up regularly by jogging along the sidelines during the game. While they are doing their physical warm-up on the sideline, prompt them to do a 'mental warm-up' recapping the key performance focus for the team and their own role. Also, reminding a substitute about his or her strengths or 'weapons' can give them an edge when they enter the fray.

Notes

1. Luckhurst, S. (2015). Manchester United: Dismissing Keane was Sir Alex Ferguson's best decision. *Manchester Evening News*, 18 November. www.manchestereveningnews.co.uk/sport/football/football-news/manchester-united-dismissing-keane-sir-10458588
2. Mottram, D. (2010). *Drugs in Sport* (5th ed.). London: Routledge.
3. John Terry racism row with Anton Ferdinand: timeline. *The Telegraph* (Sport), 27 September 2012. http://tinyurl.com/c9547oq

4. Cricket Australia 'arrogant' and partly to blame for ball-tampering, report finds. *The Guardian* (Sport), 29 October 2018. www.theguardian.com/sport/2018/oct/29/cricket-australia-arrogant-and-partly-to-blame-for-ball-tampering-report-finds

5. Sir Ernest Shackleton and the Endurance expedition. *Shackleton's Antartic Adventure.* Retrieved from main.wgbh.org/imax/shackleton/sirernest.html

6. Maraniss, D. (1999). *When Pride Still Mattered: A Life of Vince Lombardi.* New York: Touchstone.

7. Clough, B. (with J. Sadler). (2002). *Cloughie: Walking on Water.* London: Headline.

8. Ibid.

9. Clough, B. (with J. Sadler). (1994). *Clough: The Autobiography.* London: Partridge Press, p. 140.

10. Duffy, P. J., Lyons, D. C., Moran, A. P., Warrington, G. D., & MacManus, C. (2006). How we got here: Perceived influences on the development and success of international athletes. *Irish Journal of Psychology,* 27 (3–4), 150–167.

11. Chelladurai, P. (1993). Leadership. In R. N. Singer, M. Murphey, & L. K. Tennant (Eds.), *Handbook of Research in Sport Psychology* (pp. 647–671). New York: Macmillan.

12. Talking the talk. *The Observer* (Sport), 15 April 2007, p. 12.

13. McDonnell, D. (2008). Sir Alex Ferguson: I hate using the hairdryer on my Man Utd players. *Mirror,* 5 February. http://tinyurl.com/bwhuzlm

14. Yeager, D. D., Purdie-Vaughns, V., Garcia, J., Apfel, N., Brzustoski, P., Master, A., Hessert, W. T., Williams, M. E., & Cohen, G. L. (2014). Breaking the cycle of mistrust: Wise interventions to provide critical feedback across the racial divide. *Journal of Experimental Psychology,* 143(2), 804–824.

15. Guardiola 'not special' but plans to build on winning culture. *The Sunday Independent* (Sport), 12 August 2018, p. 1.

16. Marcotti, G. (2001). Made not born. *The Sunday Tribune* (Sport), 7 October, p. 9.

17. Ibid.

18. www.nelsonmandelas.com/mandela-quotes.php

19. www.rateitall.com/i-53312-john-wooden.aspx

20. Wooden, J. (with S. Jamison) (1997). *Wooden: A Lifetime of Observations and Reflections On and Off the Court.* Lincolnwood, IL: Contemporary Books.

21. Wooden, J. (with S. Jamison) (2007). *The Essential Wooden: A Lifetime of Lessons on Leaders and Leadership.* New York: McGraw-Hill.

Index

Made in the USA
Coppell, TX
08 December 2021

67517867R00126